What Other Men Are Saying About Faith For Fiery Trials

Men Impacting Men With Real, Raw and Relatable Stories

Presented by Nicole S. Mason

One of the most needed and yet overlooked narratives in society is the journey that men take on the path of becoming. Strength is demanded. Success is expected. Struggle is often silenced. What is necessary for us to build the next generation of whole fathers and sons is the sharing of the biographies of men that life has made, and the Lord has transformed into emblems of grace and faith. These discourses are the "necessary inheritances" that will turn the hearts of generations and eradicate the Malachi 4 "curse" that smites the earth because of the lack of fathers' and sons' hearts turning to each other in a profound embrace of generational legacy and anointing.

"*Faith For Fiery Trials: Men Impacting Men With Real, Raw and Relatable Stories*" is a poignant amalgamation of transparent stories of men who, harrowing life experiences, come to discover their identity, worth, and purpose by encountering the Ultimate Father, who has a preparation for all of the deliberations of life. I wholeheartedly recommend this as a needed reading for men (and women) who struggle with overcoming "struggle" and discovering true life that can only be given thru faith through Christ. No fire can destroy the man who is only tempered by the fiery heat of the flames. The promise of God is sure: We shall come forth as pure gold!

Bishop L. Spenser Smith
Senior Pastor, Impact Nation Fellowship
Church
Presiding Bishop, Unity Impact Fellowship
www.theimpactnation.org

In the true spirit of openness and honesty, the stories in this book deliver seriously real and clear messages of what it means to struggle as a man. However, the stories don't leave you in the struggle. They provide a pathway for men to walk out of the fire and into the safety of God's hands.

Throughout this powerful book, *Faith for Fiery Trials*, presented by Dr. Nicole S. Mason, you're going to see the real-life everyday struggle of real men. The challenges many of us have faced that perhaps we have never talked about and the obstacles many men face today are revealed in every story. The stories will take you on a ride of familiar scenarios and identifiable hardships by different men, but that is so often prevalent to every man in some form.

This book is a manual of commonality that ties all men together and yet delivers us individually based on the purposeful power of God. I highly recommend this book to all men to help us realize we fight better together because we are fighting against the same enemy. In seeing this bigger picture, our words have the power to help others, and this book is another tool in the arsenal of encouragement.

I would suggest you put this book at the top of your new books to read list because it provides great insight into how today's men are utilizing their faith to defeat our daily enemy. You won't be disappointed in your purchase.

Otis Robinson, Jr., Pastor
Foundation Point Church
www.foundationpointchurch.com

The stories from the men in this book are superb! The commonality is that 'something drove them to submission." James 4:7 admonishes, "*Submit yourselves therefore to God. Resist the devil, and he will flee from you.*" (King James Version KJV) Often, submission is viewed as a 'male dominance' word because Ephesians 5:22 states, "*Wives, submit yourselves unto your own husbands, as unto the Lord.*" (KJV) However, the preceding verse admonishes husbands and wives… "*submit yourselves one to another in the fear of the Lord.*" Ephesians 5:21 (KJV). The reader will discover each author had an epiphany, usually due to a female. This encounter enabled them to become God's man. *Faith for Fiery Trials: Men Impacting Men With Real, Raw and Relatable Stories* illuminates these great men!

Deacon Brad Walker, Editor 'The Greater' – The Magnificent View Magazine
The Online Magazine of the Greater Mount Calvary Holy Church
www.thegreatermv.org

Faith For Fiery Trials: Men Impacting Men With Real, Raw and Relatable Stories is definitely an interesting, impressive, and illuminating book to read. I found myself engrossed in the testimonials of the authors. I could identify with some of the tests and trials presented in this book. I happen to know a little bit about each of these men and their stories personally and know that they are good examples of Christian leaders. To see that God can change a man from his sinful thoughts and sinful ways and bring him to a place to be used by God is simply amazing.

This book is a great work! I highly recommend and endorse this book to men and women of all ages. This book allows one to see how God can use men of different aspects of life, no matter how hard or different one's life has been, and mold them into what He wants them to be.

I benefited from reading this book, because it showed me some weaknesses that God is still working on in my life now. I am even more confident that if God can progress and improve the character of my brothers in Christ, He can definitely do it for me!

Elder Robert McNeal
Greater Mount Calvary Holy Church
https://www.facebook.com/robert.mcneal.16

Elder Nicole S. Mason, Esquire, is to be commended for adding another excellent book to her collection of writings that is sure to become a best seller! This compendium of stories concerning the fiery trials of African American Christian men is what has been missing from and is much needed in Godly literature. A collection such as this brings together the story of African American men from a wide spectrum of backgrounds.

These men, many of whom I have had the pleasure of serving with in ministry, spare no details in telling a compelling story of their life's journey and of God's Faithfulness, even while they are in the midst of their struggles. I believe that this book will be especially valuable to young men whether they are Christians or whether they are in search of a relationship with God. These transparent and vulnerable life stories give the reader a glimpse of the many roads that these men have taken to establish a covenant relationship with God. Though each journey takes its own unique path, they all fall under the rubric of "Walking by Faith." Thank you, Elder Nicole!!!!

Pastor Alfred A. Holston
Hope XPress Community Church
www.hopexpresscommunitychurch.org

My first word for this book is wow! I found myself in some instances relating and in other instances just blown away. I really felt the emotions that were placed on the page. I found myself applauding and, in other moments, wanted to weep. The stories made me thank God for these men. I had a mother that watched over me and put me in situations that I could excel in.

All I can say is every man should read these stories. They are filled with courage and transparency that allows those who read them to cheer or cry. What courage it took to share their lives with us. I highly recommend this book for all men as it will encourage and embolden them. Bless you and bless these courageous men of God.

Pastor Wesley Pennington
Rally Point Men's Ministries
www.rallypointmensministries.org

I dedicate this first of its kind literary work highlighting the trials and triumphs of African American, Christian men to a Man that I, along with the Co-Authors in this book, love so much, our Pastor and Spiritual Dad,
Archbishop Alfred A. Owens, Jr.

Ordering Information

Quantity sales and special discounts are available on quantity purchases by corporations, associations, and others. For details, contact the "Special Sales Department" at the address above.

Printed in USA

Faith For Fiery Trials: Men Impacting Men With Real, Raw and Relatable Stories/Nicole S. Mason, Esquire

ISBN: 978-1-7347912-1-1

DEDICATIONS

Steve Alsbrooks

I dedicate my chapter to the people who shaped my life and had the most impact, my loving parents, Hershell and Pauline Alsbrooks. Their love, support, and guidance are the very foundations of my life. I also dedicate my chapter to my sister and friend Karen Alsbrooks and my beautiful niece Kayla Smith, who is like my daughter. Also, to the two young men I proudly call my sons, Aaron and Andrew Alsbrooks. To the love of my life, my wife Carol Alsbrooks, the mother of my children who supports, loves, and honors me daily. Last, but assuredly not least, to my Lord and Savior, Jesus the Christ. Thank you all for your support.

To my children Tamille, Raymond, Tony Jr., and Cachet, thank you for sticking by me and believing in me during the tough times highlighted in my chapter. I love ALL of you so much!

Sean P. Mason

I dedicate my chapter to the strong men in my life and those who came before me: my great-grandfather, Reverend E. B. Mason, grandfather, Crosby Adams, and my father, Royal Barrington Mason. Additionally, my maternal great-grandfather, Robert Henry, my grandfather, Theodore Ignatius Wilkerson. To my uncles, Earl Pierce, Lovey Pierce, Bobby Wilkerson, Leroy Ingram, Bill Ayers, and Ray Rogers. To my cousins, Ricky Pierce, Earl Pierce, and my favorite cousin, Kenny Ingram. To my brothers, Baron Mason, Derek Mason, and Royal Mason.

To my Spiritual Father, Archbishop Owens, thank you for everything that you have done for me, taught me, and exemplified for me! You are the epitome of a Godly Man!

Alvin Owens

I would like to dedicate my chapter to my extremely talented, hard-working, big-hearted daughter, Tykia Jarniece Owens. Your birth into this world changed my life for the better. I am so very proud of the woman you have become.

I would also like to dedicate my chapter to the memory of my Mother, Susie, and my Father, Alfred Algae. A special thank you to my wife, Barbara, for her encouragement and loving support. My son Michael Alfred who challenges me to be the best Dad I can be. My adoptive daughter, LaPria Teniece, whose beauty shines forth inside and out, and my grandkids who bring great joy to my life, Kynley Harper and Brion Ashanti.

Elder Anthony Pender

I dedicate my chapter to my wife, Helen, and my daughters, Bria and Brittany; I want to thank you for encouraging, motivating, and pushing me to write this chapter. Without your belief in me, I don't think I would have been able to do it.

Deacon Edward "Leon" Best

I dedicate my chapter to my loving wife Angie. You are my heart. You are the wind beneath my wings. To my two Mamas, who raised me and loved me unconditionally. First, Mrs. Thelma P. Best instilled the love of Jesus Christ in me at an early age. She would always tell me that I was a rich descendant of King Solomon and that royalty is in my blood. My second Mama, Mrs. Queen Gray Joyner, always loved me and made me feel like I was her very own son. The love, wisdom, and knowledge I received from both of my Mamas has been and continues to be invaluable.

I also dedicate my chapter to my sons, daughters, grandkids, brothers, sisters, aunts, uncles, nieces, nephews, and cousins. Each one of you knows the love I have for you.

To my Pastors, Archbishop Alfred A. Owens, Jr., Co-Pastor Susie Owens, Bishop T. Cedric, and Lady Bobette Brown, Pastor Kristel Woodhouse and Pastor Will Grandberry, and my Greater Mount Calvary Holy Church Family.

To my Dad, Archbishop Owens, you have had such an incredible and powerful impact on my life. I know God has ordered my steps, and I thank Him. He led me straight to you. Dad, I love you! Not just for the Man of God that you are, but because of the genuine love you have for people. Your integrity precedes you. Thank you for being the Dad I never had.

Of course, I saved the best for last: my big brother, Adrian "Pop" Powell. Even when you were a kid yourself, you stepped up and took the reins to help Ma with us. Along with your siblings, I have exceptional love for you because you were always there for us. You have always taken care of us. The family has always been important to you. I believe that's why God placed a special anointing on your life. Who would have thought as kids God had this designed for our lives. ENJOY YOUR LEGACY!

Elder Tony Keith, Sr.

I dedicate my chapter to my wife, Star, and thank God for using you to save my life. I thank you so much, and I am forever grateful to God for you.

Minister Bernard Perry

I dedicate my chapter to the legacy and memory of my daughter, Kayla Ross Perry, gone but never forgotten. One Sweet Day, Live, Love, Laugh #KaylaStrong

Russell Roy

I dedicate my chapter to my daughters, Shadae and Janae Roy. I wrote this story because I have tried my best to communicate to you that you never have to lower your standards and values to be accepted by anyone, particularly a man. You should constantly challenge people you care about to be their best, never reducing yourself to fit in or accepting mediocre standards. If you want something or someone so bad, you must ask uncomfortable questions. Never be afraid to push. It's an ingredient to your pursuit of happiness.

Linda, I thank you for your strong-willed spirit and for knowing what you wanted in life and not accepting average from me or anyone else. While your question hurt my feelings, it needed to be asked. The question actually birthed me out of myself. I appreciate and thank you for maintaining your standards.

To my Kimberly, God knew when you were in your mother's womb that you would be my wife some twenty-two years later. They say behind every good man is a greater woman. The only time you have been behind me was to push me forward or when you held me up when I wanted to give up. We have walked side by side for thirty years, and I thank you for rolling with me when I only had little to give. I pray that you realize you have a Rollie (Rolex) and not a stopwatch. I love you!!!

Deacon Daryl Shambourger

My Heavenly Father's love and life-changing Word helped me mature, overcome and endure. To my wife Nicole, you are an angel and the love of my life. Life without you is unimaginable. To my daughter Nia (M-I-T-I-D-L), you never cease to amaze me with your endless talents. I love you, infinity plus one. To the men fulfilling our many life roles, do not neglect self. We must take care of our temples to be effective vessels for Christ.

Deacon Thomas G. Wright

An African proverb reads, "*A family is like a forest; when you are outside, it is dense. When you are inside, you see that each tree has its place.*" I dedicate my chapter to the people in my life who I can now say without equivocation have played an integral part in my story. I thank my mother, my first love, and the woman whose approval was crucial to my development, whether coerced, commanded, or freely given. I thank my father. I know the kind of man he was, but the change he made confirmed that God's love is real and the Holy Spirit's power and influence in a willing vessel is undeniable. I thank my sisters who served as my protectors, confidants and then allowed me to serve as their big brother even though I was their baby brother. I dedicate this chapter to my beautiful niece and nephews. Thank you for allowing me to be a father figure in your lives. I pray I did or said something that made your life better.

God knows I thank my wife, Paula. Why the Lord blessed me with her is beyond me. My biggest fan and believer that there is nothing I can't do. Your love, prayers, and challenges are why I'm any good at being a husband, father, grown man!

Finally, I dedicate my chapter to my sons. One of God's greatest gifts He has ever blessed me with are my sons, Evan, Alex, and Christian. I've never wanted to be more successful at anything more than being a father. I've never questioned, criticized, and prayed over more decisions and actions of my life than the things that involved them.

For the trees in my life, I dedicate this work

FOREWORD

From the words of the great poet Maya Angelou, "I did then what I knew how to do. Now that I know better, I do better."

Angelou's sentiments remind me of the great testimonial stories of the ten men highlighted in this book. While this 3rd installment of the Faith For Fiery Trials Franchise book is a Men's Edition, the fact that the stories are by men, about male issues, the stories are both enlightening and inspirational for women too!

Mason, both in strategy and challenge, coached these men into sharing a small sketch of their lives that celebrate their triumphs over their defeats.

It could have been another way! But God! The memories that these men share, which were once painful to recall, are now witnesses to the transformational power that God gives to the lost but now found men of God.

I am blessed by God to be connected to these brothers by being their pastor and spiritual father. I have walked with them through both good and bad times. For sure, their good days outweigh their bad days.

It remains an honor for me to put pen to paper and congratulate these beloved brothers in Christ.

Without question, you will be blessed and encouraged when you read these vignettes. I thank these men for unashamedly sharing a portion of their lives in print, and I thank Nicole Mason for this compilation of good work that is sure to bless those who will read it.

Archbishop Alfred A. Owens, Jr.
Senior Pastor
Greater Mount Calvary Holy Church
www.gmchc.org

CONTENTS

INTRODUCTION

Emotionless and Exhausting are normal
adjectives that can be used to describe the
experience of being a Black Man in America.
Born into a toxic hyper-masculine culture where
the definition of man precedes the womb, little
room is left for many Black boys to discover
their individuality and their brilliance. In turn,
these same boys grow to formulate a system that
allows them to function as normal in the exact
society which views them as a threat. Eventually,
these boys become men and raise their sons with
similar values, not to thrive but to merely
survive. This is the reality of cyclical
dysfunction that is inherited from the trauma
passed down from generations impacted by
slavery. Since black people have been on
American soil, we have had to live in the
dichotomy of being a need while simultaneously
being hated. The only possible way for any
Black man to thrive in such an evil and barbaric
climate is with Faith. Every day, we see and

witness countless souls of Black men, but what we never discover are their stories.

We all have a story. For some, it is a testimony, and for others, it is a tragedy. Nonetheless, it is a story attached to survival. Growing up with a father who was a teenage gangbanger in Chicago was a tough act to follow. Although my dad changed his life and instilled values and principles within me, internally, I believed he wanted me to be like him. I was the complete opposite. Instead of being on the corner, I found my safe place in the church. For many, that would be considered a compliment or a statement of innocence. But there are no words that adequately express the toxic pressure of the culture experienced for a Black boy growing up in the inner-city. Anything out of the norm from the traditional patriarchal view of masculinity was viewed as strange and weird. So, the only means of survival was conformity. I had to play the role and perform, becoming delinquent and defiant. This was a tormenting reality which felt like the quicksand to every dream and promise desired. Until one day a senior from the community saw me and decided to share his story. When I heard his story, I realized that I was not alone. I also realized that I was not strange, but more pointedly, I was special. In short, a simple story saved my life.

Faith is rooted in the most powerful story ever told. An innocent Black man wrongfully accused and condemned to a cross for the sins of the entire world. However, he was raised from a sealed tomb with ultimate power over death, hell, and the grave. What a Story! Faith from the belief in that story has transformed the lives of millions of Christians worldwide. Faith is more than a religious word that is used to create hysteria on Sunday morning. More so, faith is the driving force of hope and the primary ingredient within the passion of one's purpose. However, faith is not legitimate until it is tested by fire.

In a time where the narrative of Black men has been shaped and manipulated by the dominant culture and media, Elder Nicole Mason's vision brilliantly conveys a realistic portrait of redemption that identifies with the common everyday man. This collaborative work draws us in with the transparent testimonies of ordinary men, who were born in fire, but who discovered faith in the midst of devastation, which ultimately shifted them into a refined future. I believe that this timeless piece of literature will bless the hearts of many fathers, brothers, and sons for generations to come.

The power in each story leaves any man to resolve the most refreshing theme, "***You are not alone***." We all have a story. There are no details spared describing each man's story, ranging from promiscuity, pornography, drug addictions, etc. This book is without question a divinely sharp weapon against the lie and plan of the enemy. It is the story of overcomers who courageously attest to the power of faith in every trial faced. This work is impactful, inspirational, and transformational for every man in every generation.

So, let me caution you. This is not the average book that you have purchased for shelf placement. It is not only a must-read, but a must-share. Drenched with the blood, tears, and emotions of strong Black men who vulnerably tell their story of overcoming the most challenging hurdles any human can face, this book is a classic. I can guarantee that it will do for you as it has done for me, impact your life forever. So, buckle up and prepare for this ride through redemption, which in turn will provoke hope, honesty, and most of all, faith in your own life to remind you that God has the power to do anything with anybody. Romans 5:5 says, "*And hope does not put us to shame, because God's love has been poured out into our hearts through the Holy Spirit, who has been given to us.*" (New International Version NIV) Faith proves to CONQUER ANYTHING!

In His Service,
Pastor Will Grandberry
Outreach and Community Development
New Life Covenant Southeast
Facebook.com/will.grandberry
Instagram @pastorwillg

SEAN P. MASON

I WAS A FATHER BEFORE I WAS A MAN

By the time I was 26, I had four children with three different women, a low-paying job, and an incomplete college education. It wasn't my intent to become a father before I was a man. But let me tell you, that is what happened to me. Most of the time, having sex and having a baby are worlds apart in most men's minds, but we all know that every time you have sex, there is a high probability that you can create a child. Typically, there is no conversation about having a child or the other ramifications of having sex. The problem at that point in my life was immaturity. My mission was to have as much sex with as many women without thinking about the consequences.

When I think back and look at life at that stage, there was no way that I could have had productive conversations with the three mothers of my four children. For example, who do I pick up from school? Whose recital do I attend? What day do I take the boys to the barbershop? And the real question was how would I pay for it all? So, I made a big mistake. I allowed child support to raise two of my children, so I didn't have to be a man and show up. I just paid child support every month, suppressed my feelings, and neglected my fatherly duties of being a protector and being present.

Let me tell you my feelings at that time. I was angry as hell because I had children with women that I never had the conversation with about being a father. The only control that I had was not to participate in the act. So, I felt trapped in a lifelong situation that I willingly went into. The only control is to use wisdom about your decisions. You have to communicate about your wants and desire to be a father. Remember, the consequences last for a lifetime.

Growing up around a man allowed me to encapsulate the meaning of manhood training. I was born in the late 60s, and my father, Royal Barrington Mason, is a man's man and my hero. Let me define what a man's man is: a man that takes care of his responsibilities; he's a disciplinarian; he works and provides; he protects; he teaches, and he loves his family. He works hard to study his craft, whatever his craft may be. If he does not know the answers, he seeks someone that does. He solidifies the success of his family by leaving a legacy. He also has a good reputation and is a positive influence in his community.

Although I was raised by my father and thought I understood the responsibilities of being a man, I entered college and soon realized that I didn't quite comprehend what all of being a man meant. You see, that's the thing about growing up. It is essential first to know where you come from. I hail from a long line of great men who were always there and available for me. But life will teach you that there are some aspects that you will have to learn for yourself.

When I was in high school, I followed the three things that I have heard men talk about my entire life, women, sports, and money. I loved women, and I played basketball. Now I can tell you that the only way I was going to college was on a sports scholarship. I was the youngest of six children, and my family could not afford for me to go to college. I visited a couple of colleges, and the one visit that changed my life was a visit to Howard University during Homecoming in 1985. I had never witnessed so many beautiful black women in the same place at the same time! WOW!! I made the decision that day to attend Howard University. The Washington Post reported the following week, *"Sean Mason Signs with Howard University."* I was awarded a full athletic scholarship to play basketball. I stepped onto the campus of Howard University in 1986. I spent more time pursuing the women on campus than my academic studies. Thank God for the mandatory study hall and tutors to help me navigate my classes.

I learned so much about myself and life while at Howard University. I had the opportunity to travel around the country with my team. I learned about brotherhood and how to support others. I learned about my African heritage and the many great leaders that had come before me. What an incredible experience to sit at the feet of educated black educators who were making a tremendous impact, not only in the community but in the world, with their scholarship, expertise, and experience.

What I thought was fun was building my faith. In 1987 on the campus of Howard University, I met the one woman that would change my path from young and immature to a path of faith. I met Nicole Sherron Haile. We had our first son while in college. It was a trying time because of our age. I had never held anything bigger than a basketball. I never changed a diaper in my life. None of my manhood training prepared me for fatherhood. There isn't a book or a class that can take a college student from the basketball court and develop him into a father - only time. So, I turned to the man that guided me throughout my life, my father. With his wisdom, he said to me,

"You had fun creating him so you can have fun taking care of your creation." I had to stop playing basketball and get a job. I did just that – I got a job. I didn't have a degree. I worked two jobs for nine years.

My father even gave me a car to help. But, of course, that was not enough. Our two families were such a blessing to us. I can never thank them enough. Nicole graduated and moved into her career, and I was still working at two low-paying jobs. That is when it got fiery. Nicole must have had faith in me before I did because she stayed with me, and I am eternally grateful to her for her support and love. After our first child was born, I worked, played basketball, and I was still sleeping with other women. I had two daughters with two other women. My life started to spiral out of control. I had to explain to Nicole and our families that I had two daughters and needed financial support.

Now let me talk about my experience with child support. I agree 100% that a man that has a child and is not providing financially, the court system should enforce child support. I also believe that the child support system should be reviewed and updated to ensure that the support is being used for the child. I had child support coming out of every check and still had to maintain a life. I would always get a call that one of my children needed something else. Let me warn all mothers that have a situation like this. Child support can order the father to pay a monetary amount, but it cannot make him spend time with the child or fully participate in the child's life. There is no book for a man to learn how to be mature. All of the training that I had from all of the strong men in my life taught me the most valuable lesson - never have a child by a woman that you are not married to.

After my fourth child was born, my second son by Nicole, I realized that I needed help. I started going to Church. What is amazing is God's faith in me was always there and available to me. He had never left my side. I finally went back to college and graduated from Howard University. If I were a betting man, I would bet you that I was likely the only man to graduate that day that had four children by three different women. I didn't know that I would have to take test after test to have a testimony. I eventually matured and decided to marry Nicole. So, we got married, and we had another son – The Last One! I always had faith in myself but realized that faith in God is what has kept me. There were times that I wanted to leave and start over, and I would question every decision I had to make. I realized that I had to start paying attention to my two daughters and start communicating with their mothers. I was 35 years old and knew I had to grow up and be the man that I was taught to be.

I started attending Church but believe me I wasn't ready. But when you listen to the Word long enough, you will conform to God's mercy. I really had to look in the mirror and ask myself some tough questions. Did I want to be married? Did I want to stop cheating with other women and commit to my wife? Did I want to take care of my five children? Did want to be a positive role model in my community and respect God? So, I had to dedicate my life to something. The game plan was laid out for me, my steps were ordered; I just had to take one step, and God would take two. So, I turned my life over to Christ, and although the journey has not been easy, I am on the right path. I had to really let go and grow up, accept responsibility for my actions and take care of my family. Take care of those that created you and take care of those that you have created. That is what a man does.

Recommended Manhood Rules to Live By

Never fall into the trap of drugs and alcohol.

Always listen to and honor your parents.

Dream BIG and follow your dreams.

Learn and perfect your craft.

Never abandon your children.

When one eats, we all eat.

Do not have children with a woman you are not married to.

Think about your decisions BEFORE you act.

Consider the consequences of your actions.

ELDER TONY KEITH, SR.

JUST IN THE NICK OF TIME

When I look back over my life, God has always shown up just in the nick of time. I have seen God take me from not enough, to just enough, to more than enough. This reminds me of a story that I read in 1 Samuel 30:1-19, the Bible declares that David and his men returned from war to a city called Ziklag, only to find the city had been burned with fire, and their wives and their children were taken captive. David and his men practically lost everything. The Bible says, *"Then David and the people who were with him lifted their voices and wept, until they had no more power to weep."* (1 Samuel 30:4 New King James Version NKJV) David seeks God for counsel, and by the end of this story, they recovered all, and nothing was lacking.

I, too, suffered a similar fate. The enemy stole everything from me, including my self-esteem, but thanks be unto God, like David and his men, I have gone from crying to recovery. Amid smoking crack cocaine, promiscuity, suicidal thoughts, bankruptcies, repossessions, a foreclosure, and so much more misfortune, God has always shown up just in the nick of time. At the root of any type of addiction, there is pain. Addiction can be defined as *"Any thinking or behavior that is habitual, repetitious, and difficult or impossible to control."* (See Overcoming Addictions on biblecenter.com)

When I look back over my life, I believe that my mother's emotional pain lived vicariously through me. I lived and acted out the pain and suffering of her many harmful experiences. My father physically and mentally abused her, and as I grew older, I learned my grandmother conceived her at the tender age of 16. My great-grandmother kicked my grandmother out of the house, with my mother in tow. My great-grandmother ostracized them. As a child, I had no way of knowing what was going on inside her. She lived a facade as if none of this ever happened. She continued to instill discipline and manners in me and my two siblings as a mom does.

My mom always managed to find compassion for me and my world. She came to my football games in the heat, the cold, the rain, and the snow. She took me to my cub scout meetings and even started a den of her own. My mom sent me to a private school for two years. She made sure that I had just about anything that I could ask for, but she was a hurting soul behind it all. I remember my parents rustling and tussling, and I also remember lots of yelling and crying. I remember it all as if it were yesterday. My parents eventually separated when I was 13 and divorced seemingly overnight. I genuinely do not recall any period of reconciliation; nevertheless, my parents resided in two separate cities, and it left me with the question that would nag at me for years – *"Who is watching me?"*

I was 14 years old, hurting, and I masked my pain by sharing cans of malt liquor and bottles of cheap wine with my friends. I consumed just enough to get a buzz, a euphoria that I thought was the next best thing to being grown up. I thought to myself, *"Why not?"* After all, I witnessed my parents drink liquor and party all the time before the fights began. They were not alcoholics nor addicted. What better role models, so I thought? I then started smoking marijuana, a.k.a. reefer. They call it K2 or something different nowadays. It is even legal in some states; nevertheless, in the early '70s, smoking reefer was considered fun; it would make us laugh about anything and anybody.

After smoking a couple of joints, I began to get hungry for sweets and junk food referred to as having the *"munchies"* – the desire to eat and snack. No delusions, no hallucinating, no paranoia, just fun! As time progressed, getting high became a routine weekend thing for a few friends and me. Nobody watched over me, but I eventually discovered God was indeed watching over me.

Two of my friends had older brothers. One brother sold reefer, and the other brother sold cocaine. I experienced my first "*hit*" of cocaine at 15. No 15-year-old has any business doing what I was doing. Nobody was watching over me. Well, God was watching over me. Using drugs and alcohol made me feel grown as if I had control over my life. Having a driver's license and access to my dad's car allowed me the freedom that I thought I wanted and needed. I would spend most weekends hanging out with the "*big*" boys, the guys who were older than me, and those who were selling drugs. I could smoke reefer, laugh with others, and snort cocaine like the "*big*" boys.

I thought addicts were those who used heroin and needles. I remember entering the bathroom at the neighborhood recreation center to an older teen shooting heroin into his arm and instantly nodding off due to the high he experienced. I recall standing in the doorway flatfooted, frozen, and frightened. Unbeknownst to me, the Recreation Center Director had his eyes on me and rescued me just in the nick of time. The thought in my mind was, *"Did God send him after me?"*

Growing up, I enjoyed going to concerts at the Capital Centre, then located in Landover, Maryland, where they had festival-style seating – meaning no seats on the floor. Many of the people in the arena would smoke reefer. There I was, 16, 17 years of age *"puff-puff-pass,"* receiving a joint from someone I did not know, taking a hit once or twice, and passing it on to somebody else I did not know. My thinking at the time was if I just stayed away from heroin and the needles, I would be fine. In addition to smoking reefer, I began selling it during my first year of College. I sold it to put gas in my car and to have money in my pocket. I was a black city boy in a 97% all-white Community College in the suburbs. Little did I know that I was under observation as a drug dealer.

Of course, I eventually became my own best customer. I stopped selling the drugs. I was using more than I could sell. I dropped out of the Community College, seemingly just in the nick of time. The school authorities were after me. No longer in college, no job, no money meant no more fun. Life had become overwhelming. I started using other drugs, such as speed and Phencyclidine (PCP), to get away from the thoughts of suicide, the thoughts of failure, the thoughts of loneliness, the thoughts of letting my Mom down, the thoughts of what happened to my family – while questioning, *"Why aren't we together?"*

One day, my Godmother, Ms. C.E. Greene, suggested that I enter the Army to make something of myself. To me, all branches of the service were the same. So, I went to a recruiter's office in downtown Washington, DC, and enlisted into the U.S. Air Force; and within 60 days, I found myself headed to Lackland Air Force Base (AFB), San Antonio, Texas. I had never been away from home before. Boy, I was scared, yet on the other hand, I was looking forward to starting my life over. I made this life-changing decision just in the nick of time.

I will never forget the day I graduated from Basic Training. We had a *"beer bust,"* kegs and kegs of beer to celebrate our achievement. Beer addicted - Nah! Only heroin and needles were signs of being addicted, so I thought.

After completing basic training, I transferred to Chanute AFB, Rantoul, Illinois, right in the middle of nowhere and nothing. I had a job, steady income, independence, yet still full of unanswered questions about what happened to my family. I played intramural sports to occupy my time, and after every game, it was party time – beer and hard liquor. What else did I have to do but go back to my empty room in the dormitory? Alcohol addicted - not me. Addicts are those who use heroin and needles, so I thought. Oh, by the way, I found out that I could buy reefer at a local park, so I began smoking again. As the old saying goes, *"An idle mind is the devil's playground."*

With limited thinking, I thought I would never make it back to Washington, DC again, so I asked my high school sweetheart to marry me. I had to get permission to marry from the Section Commander – what a joke. In those days, it was said, *"If the military wanted you to have a wife, they would have issued you one."* Anyway, I was granted permission to go home and marry. I flew home on a Friday morning, got drunk that night, got married the next day, and two days later I was back on a plane to Rantoul without my bride – questioning, *"What in the world had I done?"*

My next assignment was McGuire AFB, Wrightstown, New Jersey. My new wife and I found an apartment ten miles outside of the Base. We had two children in less than two years. *"Who taught me how to be a father?"* I was unsure what to do as a husband, much less a father! After all, my father drank liquor, abused my Mom, gambled, and slept around with lots of women. I did not understand my role and responsibilities as a husband and a father. Stationed miles away from home and nobody to talk to, I would stop by the NCO Club (a club on Base) for happy hour just about every day on the way home from work. I would drink until I got high – not drunk to a stupor, only enough to ease my pain. I was still searching for answers and acting out of my mother's pain, or was it my pain? Had it been my pain all along? I had so many questions running through my mind.

Three years later, I transferred to the Pentagon, Washington, DC, the Nation's Capital, *"home sweet home."* Everything was familiar, happy hour, nightclubs, reefer, and cocaine. I was

49

loving life, not thinking that was where my addiction began. Remember, addiction is "*Any thinking or behavior that is habitual, repetitious, and difficult or impossible to control.*" Because of my addiction and infidelity, my wife and I separated and ultimately divorced, just like my parents. Well, without the domestic violence. What a coincidence! Or was it a coincidence!? The same heart-wrenching questions sprung up in my heart again, "*What happened to me?*" "*What happened to my family?*" "*Why did it happen to my family and me?*"

After returning to Washington, DC, I was free to take part in as much cocaine and alcohol that I could handle. If I showed up for duty in uniform and on time, I did, and I always had an excuse if I did not. After all, it was nobody's business what I did after duty, or was it? I was home. I knew how to get around the city and where to go in private. I was one person in uniform and another person when not in uniform. My cocaine use put me in precarious places and situations. I was still searching for what happened to my family and why? No one has answered these questions for me to date. However, God began to fill the void in my life with the presence of a lot of people who became my family. I would quickly call others my family, whether I really knew them or if I had recently met them through someone else.

A few women filled my void through sex and illicit living. Cocaine and alcohol preoccupied my mind and freed me from focusing on the unanswered questions buried deep within me. Now, I am sure that what I thought was my Mom's pain was eventually overtaken by my very own. I began asking different questions, *"Who am I?" "Where am I going?"* I was addicted, depressed, suicidal. I could not believe that was me and my life, but I felt like I could not stop it or change it! I loved being in the Air Force! They provided ways and means for me to get a college education; they taught me discipline, servitude, protocol, order, timeliness, neatness, cleanliness, and safety. They taught me how to respect others, as well as myself. They taught me to honor our great country and so much more, but they could not tell me what happened to my family and me. Nor could they tell me why my family fell apart!

Many years later in my career, I was not promoted to senior NCO for three consecutive years for lack of study and preparation due to my lifestyle. What a devastating setback for me! Hitherto, my promotions were far ahead of the average time (i.e., below-the-zone Senior Airman, E-5 Staff Sergeant under four years); these things were unprecedented by black men or black women in the late '70s, the early '80s. My dream to become a First Sergeant was shattered. My goal to become an E-9, Chief Master Sergeant, before the 20-year mark was no longer attainable. Not to mention that I forfeited a significant amount of money that I would have received in retirement annuity.

My alcohol and drug use had affected me more than I cared to realize. I was still serving on active duty. I began living without any focus, direction, purpose, and I just did not care about others. I was walking through life like a zombie. My behaviors resembled that of my father, drinking, gambling, and womanizing. I began to alienate myself from others not to be hurt anymore. I was still yearning for someone to help me become a father to my children. How could something so good end up so wrong?

President Bill Clinton initiated a voluntary retirement program under the Temporary Early Retirement Authority, just in the nick of time. The Air Force was getting suspicious about my inconsistent behavior and frequent absenteeism. Because of my years of service, I was eligible for the early retirement program. I retired before 20 years of service and started working a good-paying job. I brought a brand-new car, and I could drink and snort cocaine as often as I pleased without the threat of the United States Air Force (USAF) disciplining me or, worse, dishonorably discharging me. But I was still hurting and crying on the inside.

Snorting cocaine turned into freebasing and smoking crack cocaine. Crack became my friend and my enemy all at once. My life began to take a spiral turn down, down, and down. I became a deceptive and compulsive liar. I stopped paying my bills and owning up to my responsibilities. I began to lose weight. My health declined as if stricken with a terminal illness. Two cars repossessed, a home foreclosed on, bankruptcy

(Chapter 7 & Chapter 13), all that was tangible was gone seemingly overnight. My world was upside down. I was at rock bottom. No job, no money, and no more fun – it seemed like a cycle that I had been in before.

I tried isolation. I tried substance abuse treatment centers, 28-day programs, and Narcotics Anonymous (NA), only to relapse time and time again. My hope was shattered until one day, just in the nick of time, God introduced me to a young man who had served only nine years on a life sentence for a crime he committed. God had touched his life and turned his life around and made him a better man. He invited me to the Church he attended. I heard a sermon entitled, "Breaking the Spirit of Codependency." The Scriptural reference was John 5:2-7 (NKJV), *"Now there is in Jerusalem by the Sheep Gate a pool, which is called in Hebrew, Bethesda, having five porches. In these lay a great multitude of sick people, blind, lame, paralyzed, waiting for the moving of the water. For an angel went down at a certain time into the pool and stirred up the water; then whoever stepped in first, after the stirring of the water, was made* *well of whatever disease he had. Now a certain man was there who had an infirmity thirty-eight years. When Jesus saw him lying there and knew that he had already been <u>in that condition</u> a long time, He said to him, 'Do you want to be made well?' The sick man answered Him, 'Sir, I have no man to put me into the pool when the water is stirred up; but while I am coming, another steps down before me.'"*

For 38 years, this man's problem had become a way of life. No one had ever helped him. He had no hope of ever being healed and no desire to help himself. Hope can be described as *"expectation, trust, anticipation, looking forward to,"* and desire can be described as *"wanting, longing, craving, yearning."*

The man sounded just like me. I was 38 years old with no hope of ever being healed and no desire to help myself, seriously plotting a suicide plan. After crying profusely during that sermon, I heard God clearly say to me, *"Do you want to be made well?"* With tears running down my face, a still small voice inside of me responded, *"Yes, Sir!"*

During this chaotic time in my life, I was involved in an on again/off again dating relationship with Ms. Starlean Lyons. She suggested that I look into Save-the-Seed Ministry to get my life together – her words sounded very familiar to me, *get my life together.*"

Save-the-Seed was a Christian-based program for people dealing with substance abuse and had a desire to reclaim their lives with sobriety and build a relationship with God at the same time. The ministry was located in Waldorf, Maryland, and the participants lived on the campus of the ministry while attending the drug treatment program. My decision to follow the recommendation of my then-girlfriend saved my life. At Save-the-Seed, I learned to read the Bible and began to understand God's Word. I learned that all I had seen and all I had gone through would help somebody else someday. I stayed at Save-the-Seed for approximately 60 days or so.

To continue to date Starlean, I had to go to Church with her. She was a member of Faith United Ministries (FUM), Washington, DC., where Dr. J.E. Sturdivant was and continues to be the Pastor. At FUM, God saved my soul and gave me new life and a new bride. At FUM, I learned to serve God by serving God's people. Within a couple of years, I yearned to enroll in a Christian education program. Pastor Sturdivant recommended Calvary Bible Institute (CBI), a subsidiary of Greater Mt. Calvary Holy Church (GMCHC). So, I enrolled in CBI. As my knowledge of God's Word increased, so did my hunger to serve others.

After completing my first year of CBI, the Lord led me to join GMCHC. I then began to realize that my entire journey was for somebody else. I received my Minister's license. I am now a licensed and ordained Elder at GMCHC. I did not see any of this coming, but God did! I currently serve on the Ministerial Alliance, the Divorce Care Ministry, the Marriage Enrichment Ministry, and the National Adjutancy Academy.

I formerly served as the Program Coordinator of the Prison Ministry, Reintegration Support Group Initiative for returning offenders. I also served at the DC General Health Campus, Detoxification Center, providing counseling and inspirational support to those participating in the Substance Abuse Treatment Program.

Like David and his men, God has restored unto me all that was lost. He has done and continues to do exceedingly, abundantly above anything that I can ask or think. God will show up just in the nick of time!

Resources
Narcotics Anonymous
www.na.org
818-773-9999

Calvary's Alternative to Alcohol and Drug Abuse Ministry (CATAADA House)
802 Rhode Island Avenue, NE
Washington, DC 20002
www.gmchc.org

MINISTER BERNARD PERRY

BROKEN HEARTED: GOD HELP ME TO BELIEVE AGAIN

It was a typical day in my life on July 6, 2017. I woke up early to eat a lite breakfast, and off to work, I went. I would typically text and or call my loved ones throughout the day. However, this was not a typical day because I was celebrating my 32nd wedding anniversary to my beautiful wife, Mrs. Edana Perry. We had family in town to celebrate with us. I received a phone call from my wife stating that our daughter Kayla had a mild seizure at work. So, I immediately left work

59

to go take her home. This was a normal routine for us because our daughter had been diagnosed with Juvenile Myoclonic Epilepsy at the tender age of 11 years old.

This type of Epilepsy causes shock-like jerks and twitching of the muscles, causing arm and facial movements known as seizures. During these seizures, an individual can fall, leading to severe injuries and sometimes death. As a father and a man of faith, I was trying to understand why my baby had Epilepsy. It did not run in our family. Yet, my daughter had to deal with this illness for the rest of her life. According to her doctors and the medical field, there was no cure; only medication would help control her seizures along with lots of sleep. I could not believe this; so, I began to question God, *"Why my daughter?"* *"What did I do wrong for her to deserve this?"*

I was praying, *"Take this away from my daughter Jesus; she is too young and does not deserve this. Jesus, please heal my daughter"* So, the tricky part about my daughter's Epilepsy is that she could have a seizure due to lack of sleep and not taking her medication daily. Please picture with me for a moment trying to control the sleep pattern and medicine regiment for an active pre-teen, teenager, college student, and young adult. My Kayla was a fighter. She played soccer, took dance and piano lessons, sang in the Choir at our Church, and later joined the Washington Performing Arts Gospel Youth Choir. She sang with the Washington Performing Arts Gospel Youth Choir for over ten years.

Upon graduating from high school, Kayla received a music scholarship to Morgan State University, where she sang with the Morgan State Gospel Choir. But I was frustrated and angry at God for not healing my daughter from Epilepsy. I worked in ministry at my Church, Greater Mount Calvary Holy Church, seeing God change lives and heal people, yet my daughter was not one God chose to heal.

I was a frustrated dad trying to believe that God would heal my daughter. I had to be strong and encourage my Kayla that I thought God would heal her and that she would have a powerful testimony that would change people's lives for the Kingdom. I prayed daily that God would heal my daughter. I thought God was not listening to me. But He was because, with all the accidents

Kayla experienced, God allowed her to graduate from middle school, high school and attend Morgan State University on a music scholarship. She had the opportunity to travel. She also had the incredible opportunity to sing in front of President Barack and First Lady Michelle Obama. Kayla eventually graduated from Montgomery Community College with her Associates Degree and began working a full-time job. I was so proud of my baby girl. Kayla had Epilepsy, but Epilepsy did not have my Kayla. God allowed her to live her life to the fullest. I struggled with it all but had to accept the Scripture found in Isaiah 55:8, *"For my thoughts are not your thoughts, neither are your ways my ways, declares the Lord."* (New International Version NIV) God's ways are not easy to understand; as a matter of fact, His ways are sometimes downright unbelievable.

My Kayla was starting to have some normalcy in her young adult life. We were beginning to talk about getting her own apartment and even buying her own car, or shall I say her dad was buying her a car. She was doing so well, and the unbelievable, unthinkable happened. Let us go back to July 6, 2017. As I stated earlier, it was a typical day in our household, except that it was my 32nd wedding anniversary. We all woke up and got ready for work. My son, Christian, was also home from Graduate School. He had been attending school in Boston, Massachusetts. During the early afternoon, Kayla called her Mom to say that she was having a couple of tremors and wanted to go home. My wife called me to pick Kayla up to take her home to rest. I left work to pick Kayla up to take her home to rest. We had done this routine a thousand times. This was normal in our household. So, we arrived at home and had our usual conversation, *"Baby, lay down and rest." "Ok, Dad."* Kayla asked me, *"Are you taking Mommy out for your anniversary?"* I told her, *"Yes, your Aunt Cookie, Cousin Corky, and Rennie are joining us for dinner at the Cheesecake Factory in Columbia, Maryland."* I watched her go up the steps leading to her room, saying, *"Happy Anniversary, Dad, I love you."* I said, *"Love you too, Kayla and please get some rest, Baby."* We had done the same routine a thousand times. Nothing was unusual about this day.

I left to pick my wife up from work, and we were off to celebrate our 32nd wedding anniversary with family over a nice dinner. After dinner, my wife and I headed home, arriving around 9:30 pm. I went to my room to change, and my wife went to Kayla's room to check on her. I heard my wife calling her name several times. *"Kayla, Kayla, Kayla!"* After about the fifth *"Kayla,"* my wife called me to Kayla's room. I wasn't alarmed initially at what I heard, because as I mentioned, this was a consistent routine in our home. Usually, I would go to her room and call her name, and she would tell her Mom and me to get out and leave her alone, that she was okay. I wish this were the case this time. It was different this time.

My wife was crying and calling out the name of Jesus. When I entered the room, my baby girl was pale. Her body was both cold and warm. I called 911 and began to administer CPR immediately. My son was home, but he lost it while I was trying to revive her. To this day, I remember it like it was yesterday. While I was administering CPR, I was asking God to, *"Save my daughter, please don't take her from me!"*

After about 30 minutes, my Kayla, at 26 years old, went home to be with Jesus. I could not breathe or think. I thought my heart was going to jump out of my chest. **My baby girl was gone**. My world was turned upside down. No parent should ever have to bury their child. The pain was absolutely unbearable, and it literally took my breath away. I remember asking God to take me instead of Kayla. I did not want to live; I was dead on the inside. God had used me countless times to help other children and their families to get out of some serious situations. "*Why did God not save my child?*" I was angry with God, and I did not want to hear anything about how good God was. And I certainly did not want to hear the all too familiar phrase that some of the saints like to tell you, "*You know she is in a better place.*" "*Are you serious?!*" I knew this, but I did not want to hear it.

I was angry! I felt like God took from me the opportunity to walk her down the aisle, the fun I looked forward to scaring off young men, buying her first car, renting her first apartment, listening to her sing, watching her become America's Next Top Model, and one day, experience her having her own family. My baby girl and I shared the same birthday on May 9. It has been tough for me to celebrate without Kayla being here with me to celebrate. All my milestones were milestones for her. This year, I will be turning 60, and my Kayla would have been turning 30. All of it was now gone!

I was a shell of a man who had nothing left in my tank. I was ready to give up on life, and God stepped in and began to do little things to show Himself faithful, to help me grieve, and to help me believe again. Psalm 34:18 says, "*If your heart is broken, you'll find God right there: if you're kicked in the gut, he'll help you catch your breath.*" (The Message Bible MSG) God continues to mend my broken heart and is helping me to catch my breath day by day.

Before Kayla's funeral, I met with my Pastors, Archbishop Alfred A. Owens, Jr, and Co-Pastor Susie Owens, of Greater Mount Calvary Holy Church, located in Washington, DC. Amid my family, friends, and lots of crying, Bishop Owens whispered to me that God told him that I should eulogize my daughter because I knew her best. I was stunned, but he was right. *Who knew my*

Kayla better than her mother and me? No one knew her better. So, on July 15, 2017, I did the most challenging thing in my life. I eulogized my baby girl, Kayla Ross Perry. It was a blur for me; everything seemed to happen so fast. It was only by God's grace, His mercy, and the prayers of family and friends that I was able to stand and eulogize my daughter. I was reminded of what God says in His Word, *"But he said to me, 'My grace is sufficient for you, for my power is made perfect in weakness.' Therefore, I will boast all the more gladly of my weaknesses, so that Christ's power may rest upon me."* (2 Corinthians 12:9 New International Version NIV) I was truly at my weakest point, and God showered me with His grace and mercy.

After the funeral, God knew what I needed to hear after turning deaf ears on Him. My Co-Pastor, Dr. Susie Owens, prayed and laid hands on me and told me that God would talk to me when I was ready to listen. So, God began to minister to me little by little. He used my wife after we had buried our daughter. Our grief was like a two-ton truck tied around our necks. On a typical day with tears in our eyes, my wife told me, "*I cannot do this without you.*" I was slowly checking out, and God knew I needed to hear this because He knows how important my family is to me. So, I had to push myself and ask God to help me and my family get through this tough time in our lives. Praying did not come easy for me at the time. How was I supposed to pray while in pain and upset with God? One of the many beautiful things about God is He is always there even when you do not want Him to be. God continued to hold my hand even when I told Him to let me go. It is without a shadow of a doubt that God directed my wife to sign us up for grief counseling. Going to grief counseling saved my marriage, and it had nothing to do with me loving my wife. I mentally and physically checked out. I did not want to be around anybody. I just wanted to curl up and die. I could not believe, nor did I want to accept, that my baby girl was gone.

Grief is not something to play with, and I needed help. You cannot drink enough, smoke enough, or sex enough to get rid of grief. It sometimes requires professional help. I know for a fact that grief counseling and the love of God saved my marriage and calmed my mind. I remember our first session. It was extremely emotional, and it was hard for me to talk without crying and feeling the pain of Kayla not being here with us. Grief counseling allowed me the freedom to speak about my daughter through my pain and tears. I found out that the more I talked about her, the better I felt. This is tricky because family and friends thought that if they mentioned Kayla's name that they were causing me pain because of my tears. So, I had to let them know it is okay to talk about Kayla anytime, even if I start crying. My response is tears of joy because they mentioned her name. I have encouraged family and friends to talk about her because it makes me feel good. It lets me know she is not forgotten.

After about two months of grief counseling, my wife and I decided to join grief groups at First Baptist Church of Glenarden. The groups are designed for women and men individually. The groups were critically important because they gave us both the opportunity to deal with our grief separately and with other women in her case and with other men in my case. It was my second session that God began to speak through other grieving individuals just like me. A young man gave his testimony that he had just tragically lost his 16-year-old son. I felt his pain as though it were my own son. God showed me that he could have taken my Kayla much sooner.

I was still fighting God with anger and unbelief and posing my question to Him. *"Why would you take my daughter at 26 years old?"* We also joined another grief group called Compassionate Friends of Maryland. This group is designed for parents who have lost children. In my first session, God set it up for us to meet a young single mother who shared that her daughter passed away at a specialty camp for children with Epilepsy. Her daughter was seven years old. This one shook me to my core. I felt her pain immediately and began to thank God for allowing my Kayla to live for 26 years. Do not get me wrong. Twenty-six years of age is still too young to die. But I could not imagine losing my daughter at seven years old. So, I began to thank God for the 26 years of life, even though I was still in pain and miss her greatly. I began to thank God for her life and what He did not allow to happen to her. My baby battled Epilepsy since she was 11 years old. God could have taken her in elementary school, middle school, high school, on the subway, on the bus, at a party, in an Uber, or in college. But God allowed her to transition in her home, in her bed, in the arms of her parents.

I am so thankful for what God did not allow to happen to my Kayla. Amid my grieving, God continues to love me and hold my hand. I'm reminded of the Scripture found in Psalm 40:1-2 that says, *"I waited and waited and waited for God. At last He looked; finally He listened. He lifted me out of the ditch, pulled me from deep mud. He stood me up on a solid rock to make sure I would not slip."* (MSG) I genuinely believe this Scripture. I was not waiting on God; He was waiting on me to listen to Him. I thank God for opening my ears to hear His voice again and touching my broken heart to cause me to believe again. I know I will never be the same again, and it is still unbelievable that my baby girl is gone.

God has given my family the tremendous responsibility to tell Kayla's story and to keep her memory alive by shedding light on Epilepsy and Sudden Unexpected Death in Epilepsy (SUDEP). My wife and I started the Kayla Ross Memorial Scholarship in 2017 through our Church, Greater Mount Calvary Holy Church. This scholarship is for young people pursuing education or training in the Arts. To date, we have awarded two talented young people with scholarships for $2,500 each. We celebrated her life in 2019 by hosting our first annual "*Kay Day*," which comprised a fun day with lots of activities, such as Zumba, singing, poetry, cooking demonstrations, and information about mental health, Epilepsy, and SUDEP. We also started The Kayla Ross Memorial Foundation in 2019. The Mission is to raise awareness about Epilepsy, provide scholarships, and sponsor creative arts events in the Community.

My life will never be the same, and there will be days ahead when I cry tears of joy (remembering my Kayla) and tears of sadness (missing my Kayla). I thank God for holding my hand as my Broken Heart continues to heal. I am comforted by Psalm 34:18, *"The Lord is close to the brokenhearted and saves those who are crushed in spirit.*"

Rest In Heaven Kayla Ross Perry, (My Scooterbug), Gone but not forgotten.
Love Always,
Dad

Resources
Kayla Ross Perry Memorial Foundation
www.kaylarossperrymemorialfoundation.org

Epilepsy Foundation
The SUDEP Institute Program
www.epilepsy.com

ELDER ANTHONY PENDER

FRUSTRATED FAITH

In Psalm 69:3, David writes, *"I am weary of my crying: my throat is dried: mine eyes fail while I wait for my God."* (King James Version KJV) Have you ever been in a place with God where you felt that God had turned his ear away from you? No matter how much you prayed, shouted, or cried, God was not answering your prayers. This was certainly my story for a season of my life. I felt like David; my throat was dry from all the days and nights I cried out to God. My eyes were red and heavy from shedding so many tears. My Faith was Frustrated. I was in a place where I was tired of waiting on God to answer my prayers.

I have been serving the Lord and serving as a faithful member of a church since my youth. I gave my heart to God at the age of seventeen. I accepted the call on my life into the ministry at twenty-one. I felt that I had lived a life pleasing to God. I am faithful to my wife, committed to my church, steadfast in my giving, and devoted to the service of God. When it came to a point in my life when I needed God, I knew he would be faithful to me. I learned in church that heaven would belong to me if I lived right. Well, I needed some heaven on earth. *Where was God? I was doing everything I could do. Why wouldn't God answer my prayers? Why wouldn't He come to see about me and help me with my pressing needs?* God soon responded to my questions.

There was a season in my life when money began to look a little funny. I was living paycheck to paycheck. Some of it was because I was not a good steward over my finances and what I had available to me. Some of it was just life itself. At that point in my life, the matter was critical, and it did not matter how I arrived there. I needed help. As a man, father, and the leader of my home, it was my responsibility to provide for my family. So, when it was tight, the pressure was on me. The only thing I knew how to do was pray. Yes, I did have a job and a good one with an excellent salary, but it still wasn't enough. It seemed like the more I made, the less we had to meet all of our obligations. The devil had his hand on our finances. The more I prayed, it felt like it only got worse.

I was a giver: tithing consistently and making sacrificial offerings, but there was no movement in my financial situation. I started asking more questions. *"Was my life of service to God and living right all for nothing?" "Was the Word of God inaccurate?" "How could I be serving and following the Word of God to the best of my ability and still meet with financial ruin?"* My Faith was Frustrated, but I kept on giving. I used my mustard seed-sized faith and believed that there would be a change. I did not know when, and I did not know how. I just believed that things would change and work out in my favor in time.

At this same time in my life, my father was diagnosed with cancer. I thought to myself, *"Enough is Enough." "Oh no, not my dad!"* I watched God take a man who had mentally and physically abused my mom for years and save his life. I watched God deliver my dad from alcohol and make him a servant to God and in the church. He began attending Bible study faithfully at his church. I remember vividly visiting my parents, and my father would leave us at the house to attend Bible study. He began visiting the sick at the hospital with his Pastor. My father was a brand-new man.

God had changed my father's life around. I couldn't understand why God struck him with cancer when he had turned his life around versus when he was living a sinful life. My family and I began to pray earnestly for my father. We began praying for healing and speaking healing over him. We knew God would answer our prayers. If God would not respond to my prayers and the prayers of my siblings, surely, He would answer the prayers of my mother. She is and has always been the spiritual pillar in our family. It's because of her prayers and her example that I willingly gave my heart to the Lord. My mom introduced all seven of her children to the Lord. She taught us how to pray and how to believe in God. We thought his healing was in the bag; God had to answer her prayers. But God had other plans for my father. So, after a year-long battle with cancer, my father went home to be with the Lord. I was mad with God! I questioned Him. I wanted to know, "*Why?*" I was always taught that we should not question God, but I needed an answer. In my quiet moments, God spoke to me, and He said, "*If I had allowed cancer to come in his sinful state, he would not have been ready to die. I had to save him first so that you will see him again in glory.*" I was thankful for the answer, but my Faith was still Frustrated.

As I grieved my father's death, my financial situation had not changed. And my time of trial and testing was not over. One of my dearest friends was also diagnosed with cancer a year or two later. This man helped me learn how to have a wholesome relationship with other men. Although my father was always in my life, we did not have a father-son relationship until later in my adult life. When I think back now, I believe this is why it was hard for me to develop a relationship with other men. This man taught me how to connect with other men and have a solid friendship through his love and example. I was coming out of my shell, and just like that, he went home to be with the Lord. I had to watch him go through his illness. He did not complain. He was still loving and helping others. I remember praying and asking God to heal and deliver him. God had other plans for him. Again, my Faith was frustrated. I learned in church to *"name it and claim it."* If that were indeed the case, something had gone wrong because it appeared that God did not hear me.

And, to make matters worse, all hell broke loose in my life. I received a diagnosis of Thyroid Cancer! I cried out to God and started asking him a barrage of questions, *"Wait a minute, God, was it not enough that You took my father, my friend, and You still have not answered my prayer concerning my finances?"* My faith was shaken. *"I believed You were going to heal them, and it didn't happen in the natural. Now me! What about my wife and my daughters? How will they survive without me? How about those promises you made me? I am still waiting on them!"* I could not believe that was happening to me. *"I can't have cancer."* I started calling the roll of all that I had done for God. *"I have been faithful, and I serve in the house of God. I have been an example for so many. I live a saved life."* I knew God had something in store for my life. I couldn't see it, and I wasn't sure if I believed it. My Faith was still Frustrated, but I decided something had to turn around. The first thing I chose to do was **Not To Give Up**. I made up my mind, come hell or high water, I was determined to win. Although my body and emotions were saying one thing, I had to change the way I thought. The Bible says, *"for as [a man] thinketh in his heart, so is he."* (Proverbs 23:7 KJV) I started thinking and saying to myself, *"I am healed, delivered, and set free."* I was not just referring to cancer, but I was referring to everything in my life that was not going well. Now, please understand that I still went through the process. I had radiation treatment for thirty days straight.

Every day when I went in for my radiation treatment, I would say to myself, *"I am healed."*

Not only did I say it, but I also had to start believing it. My skin started to peel. I said to myself, "*I am recovered.*" I lost my taste buds. I said to myself, "*I am cured.*" I lost the feeling on the right side of my neck. I declared to myself, "*I am still healed.*" I discovered in this process that my attitude had to change. I kept a smile on my face; I continued to encourage others while still going through cancer treatments. I made up in my mind I was not going to give up. My financial situation had not changed, but my thought pattern sure did. My body was still going through, but I always believed in God for a change. Guess what? My Faith was still not at one hundred percent, but I was still making it through. It is just like a car; you don't have to have a full gas tank for the vehicle to move.

With technology, we can see how many more miles we can go when we are low on fuel. Well, before technology, God said in Matthew 17:20, "*If you have faith as small as a mustard seed, you can say to this mountain, 'Move from here to there,' and it will move. Nothing will be impossible for you.*" (NIV) I learned in the process that I didn't have to have a full tank of

Faith. I only needed one-fourth of a tank, and I could still move the mountain.

I was determined not to give up. The second thing I decided to do was continue to Praise God. I wrote earlier in the chapter that I was brought up in church all my life. One thing I knew how to do was praise God. I declared that the devil was not going to take my praise. I remember attending a Worship Service, and I struggled with my Faith. I could not help but continue to wonder if things would ever turn around in my favor with my finances and health. I was hurting, mad, and confused, but I was determined to give God praise through it all. The more I praised God, the better I felt. I decided my praise would be my weapon to fight the enemy. One of the phrases the saints used when I was growing up in church was, *"When praises go up; blessings come down."* After my doctors released me, I remember my wife, in concern for me, telling me not to praise God too hard. She knew I was determined to give Him all I had in praise. It has been five years now since the diagnosis, and I am cancer-free!

After I completed my cancer treatment, God
began to turn things around. My prayers were
being answered, and I started receiving increases
and promotions on my job. During this time, I
served as a supervisor for about ten years. In
May of 2018, God sent an advancement my way.
My employer changed my position from
supervisor to manager. The job came with a raise
of approximately $15,000. We were doing
alright, and I was content with the advancement
and the increase, but God was not through. A
year later, I was called into the office by my
Senior Manager and Executive Director. They
informed me that they had discussed my salary
and value with the company. They decided to
increase my salary to where I would be making
over six figures! I was overwhelmed, and I felt
like shouting and praising God, right there in that
office. Let me be honest; I did for a quick
second. All this for a person without a college
degree. I knew it was God working in my favor.

In the same year, I was praying to God about my
spiritual position. I have been serving faithfully
as a Minster since I was 21 years old. When I
turned 50 years old, I felt God moving me to

another level in ministry to serve in the role of an Elder. I went to my Pastor to inquire what I needed to do to prepare myself to go before the church organization's Board of Examiners the following year. God showed up, and His favor presented itself once again. My Bishop's response was, *"Son, complete the application, and I will consecrate you this year."*

During the past five years, I also went back to school to finish my education. On May 8, 2021, I graduated with my Bachelor of Science Degree in Business Administration and Biblical Studies. To God Be the Glory!

The lesson I have learned in this process is, it's not according to our timing; it is according to God's will for our lives. In our fiery trials, we must remain faithful to God. Our tribulations sometimes will be long and hard, and it may seem that we will not make it through and will never come out. We must hold fast unto God's unchanging hand. His Word declares that *"He will never leave you nor forsake you."* (Hebrews 13:5) You will have your Faith tried by life, and you may even have Frustrated Faith, and that is okay. But what we cannot do is give up. I would say to you that **GIVING UP IS NOT AN OPTION**! Although I thought about letting go and even felt like giving up, I never did. I praise God for helping me! If you are holding on to the promises of God, Don't Give Up and Keep Praising Him. God promises us in Matthew 24:35, *"Heaven and earth will pass away, but my words will never pass away."* (NIV) I am a witness that God will honor His Word concerning you. **MY FAITH IS FREE FROM FRUSTRATION!**

RUSSELL ROY

GOD USED HER TO PUSH ME

When I look back over my life and think things over, my life is probably similar to yours, or perhaps not.

Journey with me as I share my story of how I believe my good days have outweighed my bad days. On Wednesday, May 3, 1967, I was born to amazing parents, Russell and Cordelia Roy, in Washington, DC. My parents had four children, one girl and three boys. I am the eldest. At the age of 5, my parents brought their first house in

Capitol Heights, Maryland. I am a proud 1985 graduate of Central High School.

Growing up as a light-skinned male in the 70s and 80s was not very popular. I was bullied and picked on. Being the oldest in my family with an attractive sister made my life more complicated. So, being good in football, basketball, and particularly boxing in my neighborhood was my attempt to get my peers to accept me. Regardless of the sport, I still encountered discrimination within my own race. I had to run faster, hit harder, and be able to take a hit. Worse yet, I was an expressive person. Some would say I had a 'Jeremiah' weeping spirit. I hated the fact that I could become so emotional. If my feelings were hurt, I could drop a tear or two. Being so emotional often led to people calling me a "cry-baby" or, more hurtful, a "punk." It is incredible how your body's defense mechanism will kick in when you're determined to stop a specific behavior.

I had worked hard to feel good in my skin throughout my school days. I did this by constantly trying to look my best. I wanted the hottest tennis shoes, etc. However, to do that, I had to have a job. So, I worked, helping my father collect recycled paper, metals, etc., and take those items to a recycling plant where he would be paid based on the material's weight. People didn't know that I would be with my father when I wasn't playing football on Saturday mornings. He would drive from our home in Maryland to Virginia to search for large trash dumpsters near office buildings where a variety of office papers were thrown away.

My job was to jump into the dumpsters and separate the papers from the garbage along with my siblings. Once we did that, we would take that load to the recycling plant in Washington, D.C; unload it from the truck, get it weighed, and repeat these trips to Virginia until my father made the money he needed. Frequently, we did not collect enough paper to meet my dad's goal. I would always watch my father's facial expression when we rolled the paper bins onto the scale. If he appeared frustrated or nervous, I would hide and stand on the scale to help my dad get a little bit more money. I knew this wasn't right, but I was not too fond of how the owner, an old white man, would speak to my father and sometimes yell at my siblings and me. We did this work every Saturday morning regardless of the weather and the temperature. The winter was the worst. Our fingers felt like they were going to fall off. But spending that time with our father and earning that $5 each to go skating later that evening was worth it all. I continued to work with my father during the summers as a part-time custodial worker and during the week when I didn't have football practice.

In 1983, I transferred from Bladensburg High School to Central High School. The racial conflicts among black and white students were horrible at Bladensburg during my first year in high school. In fear of my safety, my mother figured out how to have me transferred to Central High School, and boy, was I glad. However, Central had its challenges. It was known as the 'get-high' school. Fighting was not primary as students preferred to smoke weed, drink beer, and eat lots of potato chips. By this time in age, I was very comfortable in my skin and accepted by most for my personality, style, and skills in football and boxing. So, when I stepped into the doors of Central High School, I was favored by the girls, liked by some males, and hated by others. I had my eyes locked in on one specific girl. I learned that she was not involved with anyone, but she was still interested in her former boyfriend from Junior High School. After a few conversations with me, her interest was only in me. We dated from the 10th grade into her second year of college and then again after she graduated from college.

I was proud, knowing that my girlfriend was considered one of the most intelligent students at Central High School. On the other hand, I was known among our fellow classmates as being a cool, athletic, and handsome thug. I believe some assumed that the things I had acquired were attained from illegal activity, which was so far from the truth. I had a job. My work ethic just happened to be stronger than my academic attention.

In June 1985, my girlfriend and I graduated from high school. She was set to attend the University of Maryland Eastern Shore (UMES) in the fall. I planned to continue working in my clerical position with the Federal Government and take classes at Prince George's Community College.

While I desired to go away to college with my classmates and pledge in a fraternity, unfortunately, that was an unrealistic option.

My parents separated during my senior year in high school, and there were no funds set aside for me to go to college. While hoping to secure a track scholarship, I simply lost focus and interest in attending college. As the oldest son in the house, I felt responsible for keeping my government job to help ease the financial concerns my parents tried to hide. Although we did not look broke, we were. With her General Equivalency Degree (GED), my mother was a skilled economist. She was able to stretch my father's two paychecks every month to pay all the bills. Still, in her efforts to ensure her children had the desires of their hearts, she went without and could not single-handedly balance the attention and love necessary for maintaining a solid marriage. My parents undoubtedly loved my siblings and me. They just struggled to show their love for one another.

I can't say that about my love for my girlfriend. I loved her, and everyone knew it. Whatever she needed, I got it. When it was time for her to report to UMES, I borrowed my father's pickup truck and packed the truck with all her dorm room necessities. I drove her and her mother to the university. It was indeed a very long ride for me. I couldn't help but think about how I might lose her to some college student, which was probably her mother's prayer. I always felt that she didn't think I was the right guy for her daughter, regardless of how much I supported her. Well, just as I thought, my girl's attention towards me started to fade. Our conversations were different. She decided to pledge in a sorority, and my insecurities grew, and my self-esteem was shattered. But we hung in there as long as we could.

In the summer of 1987, she came home from school to go with me to the Luther Vandross and Anita Baker concert at the Capital Centre. I was so excited about her coming home. I went out and bought her something to wear for the show. She, too, seemed excited, but I could tell she had something on her mind. After Anita Baker finished her performance, we sat anxiously waiting for Luther Vandross to hit the stage. While we sat in our seats, she asked me a question that I was not expecting. She asked me, ***"What are you doing with your life?"*** This question caught me off guard. Heck, we were at the Luther Vandross and Anita Baker concert!

As I stated before, I knew she had something on her mind, but I wasn't quite sure where she was heading with this question. I believe I responded by asking her, *"Where is this coming from?"* I am sure I used some other colorful expletives. I thought I was doing ok for myself. I had a full-time job with the Federal Government. I was taking classes at Prince George's Community College. I even had a part-time security guard job. But it was something about the tone in her voice when she asked her question that angered me most. She made me feel like a loser. She had a way of making me feel less intelligent and immature. She added that we were going in different directions.

At this moment, I realized our relationship was coming to an end, but for goodness sake, not at the Luther Vandross concert! My initial response was, *"What's his name?"* In my mind, it had to be someone else. I also said to myself, *"This is some B.S.!"* You know what B.S. means. She

94

denied that there was someone else, but I had already heard that she was partying very hard on campus. I sat through Luther's performance, broken and with tears running down my face, as he sang my favorite love songs. I was in disbelief, saying to myself, "*After all I have done to show this girl how much I love her, she is trying to move on by presenting the illusion that I'm not doing anything with my life.*" At that moment, it became evident to me that she didn't see a future with someone who did not have a college degree. For the first time, she sounded like her mother. Having a college degree and being well-spoken was very important to her family as everyone had college degrees and had pledged to a Greek fraternity or sorority. No one in my family had a college degree or even knew what a Greek fraternity or sorority was. We were ordinary people who believed that you don't eat if you don't work. I knew the importance of paying bills and paying them on time. I learned how to turn .50 into a dollar. While I may have struggled to put three sentences together, she never refused my gifts or financial support. I have come to know that and believe that God used her to push me. But the pain I felt from her question crushed my ego. I felt like a loser.

For months, I carried the weight of feeling like my efforts and short-term accomplishments did not matter. I cried and prayed to God to help me with my self-esteem and to help me to find a good-paying job. God used her to push me! That question has resonated in my spirit since the day it left her lips. It has become the question of my life that keeps me motivated never to stop. If I was ever lazy, not anymore, her question even today pushes me forward.

Months following our temporary breakup, I met a young lady who would later turn my life around. When we met, I was candid with her and shared that I was in an on and off-again relationship with a young lady I had dated since high school. She appreciated my honesty and preferred our friendship to go slow. I agreed, but I knew the day I first saw her, she was the one. My heart felt like it would jump out of my chest when we met-but slow it went. At that point in my life, not much about me had changed. I was still taking classes at Prince George's Community College and working for the

National Park Service as a Clerk-Typist. During this same year, my brother Chris graduated from high school, and immediately after graduation, he joined the United States Army Reserves. I was so proud of him for having a plan and executing it. He wrote me letters every week, sharing his day-by-day Boot Camp experience. Around his third week into the training, he wrote me a letter, challenging me to join the Army Reserves. He stated in his letter, "*You can't handle this*." That was all I needed to hear. I found his recruiter's information, and I called him and asked him to sign me up.

Within three weeks, I was on my first plane ride heading to the United States Army Basic Training at Fort Leonard Wood Army Base in Missouri. I had no idea my life would never be the same after the experience. When that plane took off, I separated myself from all the women in my life, and for the first time, I focused on myself. I had much to prove to myself, my parents, and my now ex-girlfriend. I trained hard. My drill sergeants recognized my efforts and made me a Platoon Guide, responsible for leading, guiding, and accepting full responsibility of my platoon for the entire eight weeks. Holding this position for eight weeks was unusual, as it was a rotated duty.

Upon graduating from Boot Camp, the young lady I mentioned earlier was now the love of my life. But there was one more thing I had to do for her before she would accept me as her man. I had to go to church with her. I was used to going to church on Easter Sunday, but it wasn't a routine practice growing up. So, I went with her to church, and I had never seen people run, jump, and dance like that in my life. I told her that I couldn't go back to that church. I told her that I thought the people were crazy. She told me, *"Choose this day whom you will date."* Well, I went back the following Sunday or so, and I have been going to The Greater Mt. Calvary Holy Church since 1988. A couple of things happened in my life since I met Kimberly Machen, the love of my life. First, I accepted Jesus Christ as my Lord and Savior. I married Kimberly. I was then called to active duty to serve in the Persian Gulf War (Desert Storm) in 1991. I spent nearly four months in Saudi Arabia as a Military Policeman. My brother Chris and I were there together in the same unit.

Upon my return home, I continued working in my job with the Federal Government, and within a short period, I was promoted from a Clerk-Typist to a Management Assistant. Months later, I completed my Associates Degree in Business Management at Prince George's Community College. About three years later, Kim and I bought our first home in Capitol Heights, MD. In that same year, I completed Barbering School at Chamberlain Vocational School in Washington, D.C., earning my Barber Apprentice License. Two years later, I took the Master Barbering License Exam and passed it. After completing these academic goals, Kim suggested that I attend my church's Bible Institute, a 4-year program, which I did.

In 1996, I began my Biblical Studies. I was fortunate to have established a favorable relationship with my pastor, Alfred A. Owens, Jr. As my second-year instructor, Pastor Owens needed a haircut. I advised him that I was a licensed barber. Immediately after class, I found myself in his office kitchen, cutting his hair, and

I have been his personal barber ever since. Through my relationship with now Archbishop Owens, he appointed me as a Trustee of the church. In 1997, God blessed Kim and me with our first child, Shadae. I later joined the Men's Choir. In 1999, I wrote a proposal to open a Barbershop in the Church's new Family Life Community Center, and on March 18, 2000, I opened the doors to my own business, Cross Cuts Barbershop. Later that year, God blessed Kim and me with our second child, Janae.

While owning and managing a Barbershop, I continued my employment with the Federal Government. At that time, I was chosen to attend the Federal Law Enforcement Training Center Investigator's Program. After completing the 11-week training program, I became the National Park Service's first African American Special Agent in 1997. As I continued to achieve accomplishment after accomplishment, I could still hear my former girlfriend's question, *"What are you doing with your life?"* So, I enrolled at the University of Maryland University College, where I took online classes to pursue my bachelor's degree in Criminal Justice. I did that for a year, and in the interim, I was promoted to head the Internal Affairs Branch at the National Park Service. It was the most challenging job I had served in, up to that point, in my life. Having been promoted to serve in leadership positions without a bachelor's degree, the Agency's Chief of Staff thought it necessary to credential my resume if I planned to be promoted further. He presented the Johns Hopkins Police Executive Leadership Program and suggested I apply. Again, I heard that question in my spirit, and I applied. Three years later, I graduated from Johns Hopkins University with my bachelor's and master's degrees in Leadership and Management. In 2014, I became the **FIRST** African American to serve as Chief of Investigations for the National Park Service. Seven years later, I asked myself, *"What am I doing with my life?"* I said, "I'm going to retire from the Federal Government and buy a condo in Florida."

In conclusion, when I reflect on my life's journey and think about my trials and successes, that question - *"What are you doing with your life?"* - seemed to have been my thermometer throughout my adult life. When the question was first asked of me some 35 years ago, it hurt me to the core. Today, when I think about that question, I believe it was part of God's plan for my life. God used my former girlfriend to ask me the question to push me to help me see my own potential. The question has become like Scripture that pops up in my head when I'm feeling low or when my life strategies or actions become stale. That question catapults me into action. *God used her to push me*! I don't believe she understood just how prophetic her question would turn out to be in my life. God used her to push me and looking back on all that I have been able to accomplish, and the woman God allowed me to find, and the two beautiful daughters I have, I give God praise, honor, and glory for using her to ask me the question. It pushed me to be the best version of myself. I serve as a mentor to other young men, and I know with all assurance that what is painful can lead to great purpose and significant promises!

ALVIN OWENS

GOD HAD ANOTHER PLAN

I am the youngest of five children. I am also the one who always got into trouble. Out of the five of us, it seemed like I was the only one getting the beatings. I do not remember much about my father being a part of my life during my young years. I was nine years old when he left. I would not talk to him or see him again for another eight years, which was the year he died. What I remember most about those years was how hard my mother worked. I know she did the best she could in raising us.

On his death bed, my father talked about how proud he was of all of us. He kept up with us, although we did not know it. At seventeen, I thought about all the times we missed together, the football games I played in, talking about my first girlfriend, and life in general. I told myself that, at that moment, that if I ever had children, I would be the best father that I could be.

Because of that void in my life, I gravitated towards a lifestyle that should have killed me. But I have come to know that God had another plan for my life. I tried to fill the void of not having a relationship with my father with drugs. I hated being around people who smoked. Even when I was with my singing group, "The Trilites," I never thought about smoking cigarettes or getting high on drugs. However, that nagging void and space remained. I was 19 years old when I started smoking weed or pot (street name for marijuana), trying it with a co-worker. I got high now and then, mostly on weekends when I wanted to party. Then it became more and more frequent. I never intended to get involved in such a dangerous lifestyle. God kept me from what should have killed me. One day, I was smoking pot with this same co-worker when he gave me a "joint." That is what we called it back then. I did not know at the time that the pot was mixed with Phencyclidine (PCP). It was a kind of high that made me feel like I was on top of the world. It was the kind of high that led to the beginning of a destructive lifestyle of intense partying, sleeping around with lots of women, and smoking.

I was having a ball. I thought that I would never fall. I thank God He had another plan. I remember two incidents where I should have died. In the first incident, I was speeding through the city, high, with the music blasting so loud that I did not hear a fire truck blaring through the intersection at the same time. I came within inches of hitting that truck head-on. Another time, I broke my fibula when I ran into the back of a bus. I was so high I walked home, not realizing how bad I was hurt. It is only by the grace of God that I am still alive.

Because of my praying, God-fearing mother, I knew right from wrong. She made sure my brother, Michael, and I always went to church.

My older siblings went voluntarily. Perhaps that is why no matter how high on drugs I got, I always knew it was wrong.

At 24 years old, I got my girlfriend pregnant. I remembered what I said to myself when my father died about being the best father that I could. At the time, I was having too much fun to stop doing what I was doing. However, God had a plan for my life. One night while I was getting high, I thought to myself, *"This is killing you,"* but I did not stop.

Shortly after that, a night-time battle began. I had no problem during the day, but in those silent moments during the night, at three, four, and five o'clock in the morning, is when God would speak to me. Sometimes, you need that quiet time to hear the voice of the Lord. God used those quiet moments to minister to me. I was a functioning drug user. I was that person who always worked, even though I was high most of the time.

When God wants your attention, He will get it. It got to the point where I would be asleep after getting high and be awakened by a voice saying,

"THIS STUFF IS KILLING YOU." Every night, the same thing. The voice of God would say, *"THIS IS KILLING YOU; YOU'RE GOING TO BE A FATHER."* I still ignored it until the thunder of the voice drowned out everything else. I heard, *"FLUSH IT DOWN THE TOILET; IT IS KILLING YOU!"* My response? *"You're crazy; I just bought it!"*

But God would not let go. He would wake me up every night saying, *"THIS IS KILLING YOU, FLUSH IT DOWN THE TOILET."* Finally, I did. The next day I bought more drugs, and that night I heard the same voice. This time, God added, *"WHAT KIND OF FATHER ARE YOU GOING TO BE? FLUSH IT DOWN THE TOILET."* Again, I did. I flushed it down the toilet. This time, it was with more meaning because earlier that day, I found out that I had a daughter on the way.

That great news of a daughter was not enough to cause me to stop my bad habit. It was a daily battle for my mind, between heeding the voice of God telling me to stop and the voice of the devil telling me I could not. Yes, the struggle was still real. Very real.

The turning point came when I decided to go to my brother's church. I got put out; actually, carried out of the church by two of the largest, bodybuilding looking ushers I had ever seen because I had a pipe in my mouth. The pipe was not lit; I was simply holding it in my mouth. I cannot even tell you why I did it, other than to say it was my state of mind at that time. As they carried me out of the church, I could see the hurt in my brother's eyes. That look stuck with me for the rest of that week. By the way, my brother is Archbishop Alfred A. Owens, Jr. Even through that humiliation; God still had a plan. It was the first time I cried and asked God to help me.

That following Sunday, I went back to church, this time without the pipe. That day, I finally gave my life to God. I was twenty-five years old. Let me be honest; I did not stop smoking drugs right away; it was a process. Before salvation, I would find any reason to smoke. Now, instead of turning to weed, I would get into my car, take a drive, or go to the tennis court, anything that would distract me from smoking. I slowed down. Day by day, I smoked less and less and began to pray more and more until the urge to smoke was gone. I had to let go of the friends and people I used to hang out with and the places I visited. Thank God I had a praying mother. When I finally made up my mind that I did not want a life of dependency on drugs, God delivered me. I remembered the vow I made at my father's death bed, and now I was mentally ready to take on the responsibility of raising my daughter.

After I gave my life to Christ on that Sunday, I never left the church or God. I started singing in the choir and listened to the preached Word Sunday after Sunday. I see now; it was all part of God's plan and purpose for me. His promise is true; *"For I know the plans I have for you," declares the Lord, "plans to prosper you and not to harm you, plans to give you hope and a future."* (Jeremiah 29:11 New International Version NIV)

All the heartache I caused my mother, all the trials I put my family through, and all the trouble I caused myself could never stop the plan God had for me. He never gave up on me. I learned that God has no respecter of person; what He did for me, He will do for you too. Just turn your life over to Him. There is nothing you can do, no matter how bad, that God cannot and will not deliver you from. I stand firm on His promise in Romans 8:38-39, which says, "*For I am convinced that neither death nor life, neither angels nor demons, neither the present nor the future, nor any powers, neither height nor depth, nor anything else in all creation, will be able to separate us from the love of God that is in Christ Jesus our Lord.*" (NIV)

I never looked back once God delivered me from drugs. My daughter is now 42 years old, and I am so proud of the woman she has become. I have remained faithful to God and faithful to ministry, serving as Chairman of my church's Trustee Board for over 25 years. Thank God my mother lived long enough to see her prayers for me answered, for me to be saved and serving God. I was 35 years old when God called her home. I am happy I could be there for her through her sickness and not be lost in a fog of drugs.

Although I do not remember spending any substantial time with my father, I now realize that his suffering from alcoholism was a disease.

110

At the time, I was too young to admit that I was powerless to do anything to change that situation. I now understand that maybe the responsibility of raising five children in the fifties was more pressure than he could handle. I choose to dwell on the positive memories I have of my father. I remember him being home playing the piano or eating his favorite snack: cheese and gingersnaps. Although I feel his absence in my life was what ultimately put me on a path of self-destruction, God had another plan for my life.

There are many examples in the Bible of men who thought one thing concerning their lives, but God had another plan for them; look at Moses, who felt inadequate but ended up delivering the people from Egypt. Jonah ran from God but ended up prophesying to the people of Nineveh. Joseph, who was sold into slavery by his brothers, but ended up in charge of the land of Egypt, and many others.

If you are one of those who can relate to my story and think that there is no way out for you, remember God has a plan for your life. Make no mistake; it is not easy because the devil never gives up. But you can do it, just ask God to show you and then let Him lead you. You do not need to be a person of great prayer; I never considered myself to be a man of great prayer, but just keep praying and calling on the name of Jesus. He will hear you and answer your prayer. I am a living witness of what the grace and mercy of God can do.

Resources
Narcotics Anonymous
www.na.org

Calvary's Alternative to Alcohol and Drug Abuse Ministry (CATAADA House)
802 Rhode Island Avenue, NE
Washington, DC 20002
www.gmchc.org

STEVE ALSBROOKS

PRAYING THROUGH PORNOGRAPHY: A THORN IN MY FLESH

My prayer is that my story will give people some idea of what their lovers who are addicted to pornography may be going through and possibly give them some idea of how to deal with it all. Although I am not proud of this part of my life, I believe it is necessary to help others get free. Also, maybe just maybe, it will help someone manage this thorn in the flesh. In 2 Corinthians 12:7-9, the Apostle Paul wrote, "*And lest I should be exalted above measure by the abundance of revelations, a thorn in the flesh was given to me, a messenger of satan to buffet me, lest I be exalted above measure. Concerning this thing I pleaded with the Lord three times that it might depart from me. And He said to me, 'My grace is sufficient for you, for My strength is made perfect in weakness.'"* (NKJV)

When I was in college, a friend took me to his sister's house for food and fun. While we were there, my friends and I went to the basement where they had some X-rated movies. We watched the movies, and I was hooked immediately. These videos gripped my soul and opened terrible doors that led me into multiple levels of perversion. Like any other kind of deliverance, I must remain vigilant about my deliverance. In the 1980s, I can recall driving to X-rated video stores and renting videos to watch at home. The other way to view the movies was going to a movie theater or a "peep show," where you could go to a shop, and they had little private booths that you could view the movies for a fee. The places that I would frequent were located on a strip in Washington, DC, known at the time for prostitution and other illicit activities. These places were terrible, filthy, and nasty.

I can recall going to one shop where there was a live show and there were X-rated movies playing at the same time. I remember sitting strategically in a seat by myself where I could see the women who were dancing live and seeing the film all at the same time. I also recall going to a place that was a sex toy shop in the front, and in the back, they had private booths that you could go into and view four different movies. You could see just about anything you wanted to see.

When I would watch these movies, I remembered everything about the scenes, as if seared in my mind. Some may ask, *"Why are people interested in X-rated movies?"* Let me give you some perspective on the question, especially to the women in a relationship with a man who currently watches pornography. When I watched these movies, it was about voyeurism and sexual gratification from watching others having sex. Unfortunately, watching pornography is how I learned about sex. As I've come to know it now, it is the way that tens of millions of people learn about sex. However, **PORNOGRAPHY IS A BIG LIE!** Most of the action you see on the screen is edited, deleted, and retaped after all the parties have rested. I remember viewing an interview with a woman who was a pornography star who was asked if she performed the sexual acts from the movie in her private life with her significant other. And she stated that the sexual acts that she performed in the film were work and acting. What she did at home with her significant other was nothing like what she did at work. When young men and women view these movies, they see a lie.

FOR INDIVIDUALS WHO HAVE NOT VIEWED PORNOGRAPHY, PLEASE DO NOT OPEN THAT DOOR! The frustration is that there is something that you are addicted to, and you cannot tell anyone. Pornography is a portal that opens in tens of millions of men's and women's lives that often cannot be closed. **PORNOGRAPHY IS A PORTAL THAT WILL EVENTUALLY LEAD YOU TO PERVERSION**. This portal allows the devil to enter your soul. While dealing with this demon, one can go through extreme frustration. *Why is* *there frustration*? For me, I could not speak about this issue to anyone because of the embarrassment, shame, and perceptions of being a Christian man. The yoke of bondage was not being destroyed. The most challenging part of dealing with pornography was that I could not find help in the church either. There are not many church organizations that deal with or speak of pornography.

Additionally, the lies that we are taught watching these movies causes frustration when you cannot find a sexual partner willing to partake in the sexual acts viewed in the movies. Being sexually aroused to the highest levels and not quenching your sexual thirst because your sexual partner is speaking a different language when it comes to sex causes frustration. This is happening all over the world. Today, many young men are involved in pornography and have expectations of having "porn sex." This, in turn, is causing more young women to watch pornography in an attempt to please their sexual partners.

The thorn of pornography attacks the mind. It is the thought that happens first. People who watch pornography have difficulty casting down vain imaginations. I can remember scenes in movies that I saw one time twenty years ago. Frequently, I would see women who would somehow trigger my mind and make me think of a scene that I had seen in an X-rated movie. Sometimes it would be a commercial or dialogue of a woman talking and acting sexy. There are many triggers, and yes, I had it bad. An old saying is, *"An idle mind is the workshop of the devil."* This cliché is so true. One way that I deal with this issue is to keep my mind focused on something else. It is crucial for me to focus on God, His Word, praying, and listening to praise and worship music. I also have healthy hobbies that I participate in that cause me to stay focused. The battle that I deal with is the high level of shame, and believe me, the struggle is real.

I used to tell myself that I am not hurting anyone and that this is a victimless activity. I later realized that this is another lie that pornography tells. The first victim in pornography is the person who participates in it. The second victim is your sexual partner. The third person that is offended is Christ. He is crucified afresh. People who are addicted to pornography spend many hours watching. I can remember watching two and three hours at a time. One thing that we can never do is get time back. **BE CLEAR ON THIS, WHEN YOU ARE ADDICTED TO PORNOGRAPHY, YOU CAN NEVER GET ENOUGH OF IT!** I have seen sex and pornography-addicted men do deeds while they were at work that could have caused them to lose their job. It can take over your life.

By the time I met my wife Carol, I had given my life to Christ. However, I still had those silent demons in my mind. At that time, I had ended the practice of going to view X-rated movies. Before we got married, she and I talked about all the issues we would bring into the relationship. It is crucial to have those hard conversations with your future spouse. We did not have a difficult time when we first started to date. We dated primarily via telephone and at church.

After we were married, one major problem was my strong appetite for sex. It far exceeded hers. She was also much more conservative in her approach to sex. But by the grace of God, we learned to compromise with one another. My wife is a woman of prayer, and she did just that –

SHE PRAYED! She also researched how she could accommodate me better sexually. And she drew the line on the things that she would not do. These were not easy conversations for us to have. But we were committed to each other, and we were very intentional in pleasing each other sexually. I learned through the process not to be a selfish lover. I have found my freedom and deliverance in God and staying focused on God, applying the Word of God to my life, praying alone and with my wife, and filling my time with other purpose-filled activities. I am clear that the lure of pornography is always lurking, and I have to remain vigilant against it. If not, I could easily be back in the grips of it with a blink of an eye. As I mentioned earlier, pornography is a door better left closed from the beginning. God did not remove the thorn from me, but I have come to know that His grace is indeed sufficient for me. This simply means that I need God's grace every day to stay focused and not slip back into old habits. 2 Corinthians 12:9 says it best, *"Therefore most gladly I will rather boast in my infirmities, that the power of Christ may rest upon me."* (NKJV)

If you or your spouse are dealing with the demon of pornography, I want to offer the following to you: (1) You must understand that you are dealing with a devil that has multiple levels and multiple doors. The first level I call soft pornography or soft porn – a low-level form of pornography. This is your everyday television show and movies. The second level is what I call regular pornography. These are films that show sexual content, except for penetration. The third level is hard pornography or X-rated pornography. This level of pornography could show almost any and everything. There are also multiple doors of pornography. For example, same-sex, heterosexual, bi-sexual porn, animal on human pornography, and it goes on and on. There are deep depths of pornography that one could dive into and see anything.

If your man is addicted to pornography, these may be some things he may be looking at on the internet. Ladies, these are the things you are competing with, your man's mind and his time. Understand ladies, no matter what level or door he is at, in most cases, this is normal to him. And he desires to have his woman meet him at his level. You may ask yourself how can I help? I am glad you asked, (1) attempt to meet your lover's needs as best as you can. He may need to meet a counselor to help talk him through his issues. You must have a prayer life to ask God to help save and deliver him. Communication is key. Having conversations around this issue will not be easy. Be persistent about discussing it with your spouse. Just know that with this addiction, the flesh is never satisfied. It will take a combination of these things and maybe more.

You do not have to feel bad because your spouse is spending time away from you. It is not necessarily the case that your spouse is not attracted to you in most cases. They are attracted to that unquenchable beast. They may tell you anything and say that they are not attracted to you, so they will not have to tell you the truth. The truth may be that they cannot stop and don't want to stop. If your spouse is addicted to pornography, you must war for your relationship. Go to therapy together. If your spouse does not go, go for yourself. Also, the spouse who is addicted needs a relationship with Jesus Christ. Pray for their salvation and believe God to answer your prayers for your spouse. I know what prayer can do, and I thank God daily for my wife and her prayers for me.

Resources

www.wikihow.com
How to Help Someone End a Pornography Addiction
Co-Authored by Trudi Griffin, LPC, MS

www.webmd.com
Pornography Addiction: 5 Treatments That Are Proven To Work
By Neha Kashyap

www.healthline.com
Everything You Need to Know About Pornography Addiction
By Ann Pietrangelo

DEACON DARYL SHAMBOURGER

STOP IGNORING THE WARNING SIGNS

Throughout my life, I have dealt with crushing pains of disappointments. Upon examining my life, my faith in the Lord has helped me overcome the many challenges that I have faced. God's grace has brought me through countless situations. It was this same faith I needed to lean on after the Lord spared my life in August 2019.

It was a traveling day! I remember the day vividly. My wife and I were excited about going to Martha's Vineyard. We planned and prepared a year in advance, and we were ready. Although our church theme declared 2019, *"The Year of Victory,"* it didn't feel much like a victory to me. I had challenges professionally that left me reeling. There were many detours and disappointments. A week away was a welcome opportunity for rest.

During our layover in Boston, I remember volunteering to stay at the gate with our bags while my wife and our travel companions went to grab a bite to eat. I had prepared a meal before we left home, so I ate that instead. When I went to throw my trash away, I felt nauseous. I discounted those signs and attributed them to a lack of rest. We had left home at 3:00 am to travel to the airport, and like always, I waited until the last minute to pack.

We continued our journey, soon arriving at our destination. Another sign revealed itself; I experienced a loss of physical strength. I felt weak loading my luggage into the passenger van that would take us to our lodging. My conclusion to this was just a result of not feeling well earlier in the week. The previous Sunday, I felt under the weather and chose to go straight home after church service and take a nap. Having gone to Urgent Care the next day, the doctor said, my symptoms appeared to be due to a viral illness.

In reality, my health was deteriorating; I had suffered a stroke. Though I had no facial drooping, all the signs were present. However, I was not paying attention. Too narrowly focused on everything else, I slowly began losing control of my physical faculties.

In marriage, two become one; there should be love, honor, and submission. For better, for worse, in sickness and in health, in joys and in sorrows, until death do us part. We vow to one another under God, and I thank God for my wife and our union. I remember in pre-marital counseling discussing the topic of studying our spouse. We are in tune with one another. She could sense things were not right.

My wife Nicole continually asked if I was okay, and my reply was, *"I just need to get some sleep."* After unpacking, uncharacteristically of me, I went to bed early that evening. It was not until the following day that she knew something was indeed wrong. I was sleeping more than usual and walking with an irregular gait. She wasn't having it and said, "*We're going to the hospital!*" In my mind, I didn't want to ruin our vacation that had just begun.

After a battery of physical tests, it was vividly clear. My bottom jaw dropped when the doctor informed me that I indeed had suffered a stroke. He could not confirm all that occurred. I needed additional tests. I don't quite remember what the doctor mentioned after that, because everything went blank. Something serious had transpired, and I needed to be transferred to another hospital to stop my health from deteriorating further.

The following day, I was transferred from Martha's Vineyard Hospital to Massachusetts General. The doctors confirmed I suffered a stroke and that one of the signs of a stroke was lack of sleep. I felt foolish. In hindsight, all the signs were right there. I thanked God for keeping me and sparing my life despite myself. I went to bed that night with the thought that things could have been over for me the previous night. I was shaken.

I thanked Nicole for being so persistent. I actually listened to her. All of my feelings of disappointment in 2019 became secondary. The Lord spared my life. I had suffered a stroke during the layover, boarded a plane, traveled to our home away from home, and went to bed later that evening. The year 2019 was my *"YEAR OF VICTORY!"*

The next several days of hospitalization were interesting. I felt like the doctors talked about me and were not talking to me, as if I were not alert. It took some getting used to having multiple people coming into my room several times a day. Of course, my doctors and I had conversations. However, I wanted to make the extra effort to let them know I was aware of everyone in the room at all times. I understood the procedures and exams: blood tests, electrocardiogram, echocardiography, MRIs, and ultrasounds. It was a blessing to have Nicole by my side the entire time.

The Lord kept my mind and my speech. I desired to make the doctors aware that I was lucid. My doctors were preparing to discharge me to an inpatient rehabilitation center. *But God!* Instead of being sent to the rehabilitation center in Boston, Massachusetts, I was released to return home to Washington, DC, and begin rehabilitation at that time.

Having the stroke was a defining moment. Although the doctors did not determine the origin of the stroke, I recovered enough to be discharged from the hospital. We began the task of scheduling all necessary follow-up appointments once we returned home. Nicole and I began to research, check appointment availability, and strategize to meet with my physicians, neurologist, and therapists.

The therapist, Sarah, conducting my intake appointment, noticed I was not using my left side. Yes, that was the side affected, and use of that side was nearly impossible, but I made no attempts to use the left side of my body during our discussion. Sarah stressed to me that, *"The brain can heal itself after a stroke, which is triggered when a blood vessel in the brain gets blocked or bursts. However, brain cells that are damaged are not beyond repair. They can regenerate, but if you do not use the left side of your body, your brain will shut that part of your body off."*

From that moment, I was in a *"combine state of mind."* What is a combined state of mind, you ask? It's a week-long event where football players perform a battery of physical and mental tests in front of coaches, general managers, and scouts. I prepared myself for the rigorous therapy tasks, highly anticipating and fully intending to make a complete recovery.

Sarah shared that my behavior and mental approach to recovery was in my hands. The Lord did His part in sparing my life, and it was time for me to do mine. Philippians 4:13 says, *"I can do all things through Christ who strengthens me."* (NKJV) It was time to get to work.

My prayer focus became intentional about pressing beyond my limitations. Of course, my diet changed; I focused on a more plant-based diet and eliminated coffee (and I LOVE me some coffee). I began monitoring my blood pressure before and after workouts. I was making progress, and the MedStar Health staff were very accommodating with appointment scheduling.

Since I was not working, the co-payments could become a financial burden. The hospital staff made concessions that allowed me to schedule physical and occupational therapy on the same day, twice a week. What a blessing!

The more muscles I was able to engage, the more it would challenge my heart and cardiovascular system. Instead of building cardio only through workouts, I weaved strength days into my training which led me to attend church service again. Live streaming was great, but I needed to be inside the church.

The Sunday I returned to my church, my Co-Pastor, Dr. Susie Owens, was preaching. Her message was so on point, and I wanted to walk up for the altar call. I decided not to out of an abundance of caution. The Holy Spirit must have spoken to one of my fellow Deacons. Deacon Hawkins walked to the rear of the church and motioned for me to *"come on."* I was hesitant, but I made my way. It was beautiful being *"home"* in church. I overwhelmingly appreciated the outpouring of love and support from my church family.

Everything was trending in the right direction until I started having thoughts of relapse. I began to experience difficulty sleeping. My progress with rehabilitation had not declined. I would wake up in the morning checking my face in the mirror. *Was my vision blurred? Did I feel any signs of vertigo or light-headedness?* I also began checking for paralysis and instability out of the normal.

For several days, I was in a cloud. Things became "*grey*" in my head. Nicole, my daughter Nia, and my family were amazing. My support group was intact; nothing changed. I was just having moments of worry. I researched so much information and was likely on information overload. I was reminded of the Scripture found in Proverbs 3:7, "*Do not be wise in your own eyes; fear the LORD and shun evil.*" (NIV)

My focus shifted. I began trusting myself and not trusting the Lord. I spent a significant amount of time on the computer researching stroke recovery methods. I needed to spend more time with the Lord. I thank the Lord for pulling me aside during those moments of emotional struggles. My trials became a purifying fire.

When those negative thoughts would come to my mind, I would anoint my head with oil. I would spend time with the Lord. I would pray over my mind, change the atmosphere with worship songs, and listen to sermons. Often, I found myself shouting throughout our home, "I WILL LIVE AND NOT DIE!" The Word is clear, *"But all who listen to me will live in peace, untroubled by fear of harm."* (Proverbs 1:33 New Living Translation NLT)

Though I have found myself in many social situations and have been a sociable person, I prefer to keep to myself. This health scare helped me to communicate more. Discussions with my wife about my feelings were more in-depth. Though I would read Scripture daily, my thoughts were still negative and unproductive.

Planning the next course of action for my life every time those thoughts would come, I would give it over to God. My focus shifted to tasks and goals set for personal and professional growth with God's help. I desired to participate in a 5K Walk & Wheel event. It was a great goal, but my therapist Lisa walked that idea back; my body was not quite ready. I craved fellowship and began developing a rapport with a few people and attending therapy sessions. As I accomplished more, my sessions became increasingly difficult. I needed a more significant challenge. I felt I was plateauing. My therapists' team helped me achieve heights I did not think were possible. During therapy, I pushed to work and challenge myself. My body was responding. Washing the dishes and loading the dishwasher were significant accomplishments. Applying deodorant using my left hand was a tremendous feat. My balance was improving, and walking daily helped develop stamina, strength, and endurance.

Eventually, I was cleared to walk without the use of a cane. Hallelujah!! Now the next goal was driving. I found it difficult to receive help in this area. Often, I would figure things out and make things come together. During this season, I had to learn to receive help. By nature, I am a giver; I have a servant's heart. Realizing that I needed to rely on the support of others was an area of opportunity. Past unsatisfactory outcomes and difficulty dealing with unfulfilled promises and expectations shaped my thinking. Being self-sufficient was just fine by me. Taking personal inventory during this season was a blessing and breakthrough. Besides, I had to rely on Nicole, Uber, or other brothers, who were kind enough to drive me to my appointments when I was in need. After I suggested trying to drive myself, Nicole hid my car keys. She knew I would not ask for help. But the day would come, DRIVING SIMULATOR DAY! I hoped to get back to normal or as close to normal as the Lord would allow. Hallelujah!! I passed and was cleared to drive.

I was moving in a forward direction and hoped that greater was on the horizon; I knew that I had a purpose and a bright future. God wanted me to grow in Him. I embraced the fact that the Lord is the giver of vision, and with God, my future was secure.

This difficult time helped to strengthen my faith. While still in the process of going through this trial, I sought God for direction. I was limited in my thinking of what He had in store for me in my own strength, but when I continued to lean on Him, I would land in the exact place where He wanted me. *"For I know the plans I have for you, declares the LORD, plans to prosper you and not to harm you, plans to give you hope and a future."* (Jeremiah 29:11 NIV)

Discovering strange things about my body much later in life and knowing that a tiny blood clot the size of a mustard seed helped transform my life was quite overwhelming for me. I was able to celebrate the fact that the Lord spared my life, and He was using me and my progress as a witness to so many others of what God could do. I was so grateful to God to share with others who may have needed to hear my story.

My faith in God helped me throughout this experience. He was an architect making sure everything went smoothly. I could not say anything about my progress without giving the Lord all the credit. I cried the day I was discharged from therapy. It had been months, and God was with me every step of the way. One of the most critical things with strokes is that people need to recognize the symptoms immediately to get to a hospital and receive the professional help required so that medical professionals can give time-sensitive treatments.

It's crucial. Otherwise, too much time passes, and much brain tissue dies.

While my medical care was unparalleled, I believe my secret weapons were my faith, family, and friends converging to lead me from trials to triumph. Every day is better than the last and always getting better. You can always get better. By sharing my story, I hope to spread awareness. I also want people to learn the signs of stroke and call 911 immediately. If you or a loved one are going through rehabilitation, have faith and stay positive.

Resources
Stroke Symptoms
By learning and sharing the F.A.S.T. warning signs, you just might save a life from stoke.

F - Face drooping
A - Arm weakness
S - Speech difficulty
T - Time to call 911

www.stroke.org

DEACON EDWARD "LEON" BEST

GOD GAVE ME TWO JUST IN CASE YOU NEEDED ONE!

It was the Fall of 1988, and the drug dealer I was riding with pulled into the Greater Mount Calvary Holy Church's parking lot. Just known as 640, the address was a notorious apartment dwelling where people sold crack cocaine in the Northwest quadrant of Washington, DC. The apartment was across the street from the church. The church at that time was known as *"The church in the hood that will do you good*!" As my drug dealer "homie" went into the apartment building to get the package, I waited in the car. I was strung out on crack cocaine, homeless, and living in a crackhouse. The basement door of the church opened. I looked over and realized that I recognized the brother standing there. His name is Caralis Kimbrue. Approximately three or four years before that day, Carlis and I were bike couriers. My brother Stan, my cousin June and I were bike couriers. We formed a racing team. We called ourselves "The Rat Patrol." We were fast! I don't mean to brag, but we were the fastest bike couriers in Washington, DC. We have the medals to prove it! In a non-stop race from Baltimore to Washington, DC, known as *The Baltimore Boogie*," I came in 1st place, Stan in 2nd place, and June in 3rd place. The timed completion, one hour and fifteen minutes. FACTS! Caralis was also an avid photographer who had taken pictures of us. That day, as I stood there, I was dirty, stinking, strung out, and weighing approximately 100 pounds, soaking wet!

The last time he had seen me, I was cut up like an athlete. Hidden behind the car's tinted windows, I contemplated whether to get out of the car and speak to him or not. I wanted to get out, but I didn't want him to see me in my condition. *How could I let him see me like this?* It was the Grace of God that spoke to my spirit, moving me to get out. He began to smile when he recognized me. We dapped and hugged. He asked, *"How was I doing?"* As I was responding, *"fine,"* I stopped, looked at him, and said, *"No, I'm not. Look at me! I started to stay in the car. I didn't want you to see me like this."* Still smiling, with this assuring look on his face, which I believe was the glow of God, he said, *"Why don't you come to church? This is a good church."* What's powerful about this is that the church has a drug program. It is called the CATAADA House. He never mentioned the drug program. Instead, he invited me to church! I remember telling him I would be in the crackhouse smoking, and God would speak to my spirit, saying, *"You need to go to church."* After I told him this, he looked at me, saying, *"It's no coincidence you're here today."* I agreed with him. I had that exchange with him on a Wednesday. I told him I would be at church that following Sunday.

Saturday nights were always busy at the crackhouse. Sometimes, I would smoke the entire weekend continuously. This is not an exaggeration. I would smoke for 48-72 hours without sleep. My drug addiction was one of the devil's plans to kill me. BUT GOD BLOCKED IT! THANK YOU, JESUS! That Saturday night, I told everyone in the crackhouse that I was going to church the following morning. Without knowing what I was doing, I later learned that I was applying Scripture to my life. The Bible declares, *"Death and life are in the power of your tongue."* (Proverbs 18:21)

The crackhouse was a basement apartment that did not have any windows. I kept hollering out, *"What time is it?"* With the pipe still in my mouth, I heard someone say, *"It's about five."* Of course, that was 5:00 am. Immediately, I dropped the pipe and ran out of the door. A crackhead leaving while there is still crack to smoke is unheard of. But God heard my prayer. I knew satan was going to try to keep me at that crackhouse because there were other times I had intended to go to church. There would be so much crack to smoke, and I wouldn't leave.

The church was about four blocks away from the crackhouse. I arrived at the church that morning and pulled on the door, and it was locked. God has blessed me with a sense of humor. So even in my dilapidated state, I looked up to the sky, arms up, and said, *"Lord, I thought the doors of the church are always open!"* Then satan spoke up, *"Okay, you've tried. Now let's get back to that crack."* As I was walking back to the crackhouse, the Spirit of the Lord said, *"Stop! Sit here on this corner facing the church and wait for someone to go inside the church."*

Leaving the crackhouse was not an easy choice for me. I could either go back to the warm crackhouse and smoke to my heart's content or sit there in the cold balled up in a knot. It was November, and I had on the same dingy, dirty t-shirt and jeans that I had worn the entire summer. I didn't have a coat, so sitting in the cold was an extreme challenge. I thank God for a praying Mama, Grandma, and big sister. Sonia, my big sis, is a "prayer warrior." She was always talking to me about changing the way I was living. She was always letting me know that she was praying for me. Of course, I didn't want to hear it. The way she would say things, always smiling, I couldn't get mad at her. I thank God for the other influential family members I stayed with as a child. They all had one thing in common. They would tell me, "*You are going to church!*" It was not an option or a choice. It was an order! Remembering those moments in my life, I balled up and sat on that corner. Even during my drug addiction, I could tell the difference between God speaking instead of satan speaking to me.

I don't know how long I sat there because it didn't matter. I wasn't moving. Eventually, I saw a guy walking up to the church. I ran the half of a block up to him. (Okay, I'm back) After I wrote that last line about running up to him, I became overwhelmed. The tears started pouring out, and I had to stop typing. I walked away from the computer and began PRAISING GOD! It was never my intention to include this part of my life. I feel God wants me to be all the more transparent. He truly is AWESOME! I have remained overwhelmed and in awe. All the glory belongs to Him!

The brother I met that morning at the church was named Cosby Kitrell. I told him that I was on crack and wanted the Pastor to pray for me. He said, *"Come on in,"* with this big warm smile on his face. He left me in the sanctuary sitting in a pew by myself. My first thought was, *"I know he knows that crackheads steal, and he's leaving me by myself*?!" But what happened next was totally unexpected. I fell into the most peaceful sleep I had in months. It was as if God was telling me, *"You can rest now son, you're home."*

I woke up to people filling up the church. They were smiling and speaking to me as they took their seats. The love I felt from those people is unforgettable. Not one person turned up their nose or moved away. When you don't feel good about yourself, you notice how people react. That day, I know I smelled horrible! Not smelly, stinky, but horrible! Yet those people showed me love and compassion. A simple smile can change a person's life. It did mine. I have learned not to turn my nose up or look down at people. I've been there. And yes, my addiction was my choice.

Nevertheless, anyone who's reading this and looks down on others with such thoughts and comments like, *"They can get some soap and water." "They don't have to smell like that!"* I leave you with this…*"But by the grace of God, it could be you."* As I looked around the church, I still didn't want to be there. *Why didn't that guy tell the Pastor that all I wanted was prayer?* I could have been long gone before the people started to come in. Well, let me tell you what happened that day. The pastor, Bishop Alfred Owens, Jr., said, *"Today, God is leading me to talk about crack cocaine."* I could not believe what I was hearing. You know how people say, *"That sermon was just for me."* He went on to say that he did not have any experience with drugs or alcohol. He felt God leading him to preach about it! *"Did that guy tell him that a crackhead was at the door when he opened the church?"*

I listened as he started to preach. And then it happened. Although I was in a discombobulated state from the drugs, not eating and sleep-deprived, let me tell you about a miraculous, healing, saving God Who can reach down through any state you're in and pull you out. At the church, the pulpit was only one step up from the floor. Bishop Owens stepped down and proceeded to preach from the floor. I didn't hesitate or wait for the altar call. I got up from my seat and walked straight to Bishop Owens. I told him that I was on crack cocaine and needed help. Again, I've had to stop typing because the tears keep filling my eyes. They are tears of gratitude and thankfulness! GOD IS SO AWESOME!

Bishop Owens put his arms around me and never stopped preaching. I remember hugging him tightly, burying my face on his shoulder, tears pouring from my eyes, just like they are flowing now as I write this chapter. I was hurting. Not to mention the loved ones and the people I had hurt. I had my arms tightly around this man. But it did not seem like he was a stranger, nor did I feel embarrassed. It felt as if I was in the arms of Jesus. So, I held on even tighter! I still remember the huge wet spot on his robe from my tears. One of my favorite Bible scriptures is about the woman with the issue of blood found in Luke 8:46, *"But Jesus said, 'Someone deliberately touched me, for I felt healing power go out from me.*'" (New Living Translation) I equate that story with me touching Bishop Owens that day that changed my life.

God delivered me from drugs in January 1989. I started with marijuana (weed), angel dust, love boat (PCP). Then came the pills: black beauties, red devils, valiums. My drug habit then included acids, LSD, purple haze, orange sunshine, Mr. Natural. I then graduated (if that's what you want to call it) to shooting drugs for the first time in Lorton prison. Two pills called "Ts" and "Ps" were crushed, cooked, put into a syringe, and injected into your veins. I still have no idea what the pills were intentionally designed for.

When I came home from prison, I tried shooting up with Dilaudid (In the streets, it was called Delaughta), big pink (Bam), Heroin (Heron), and Cocaine (Girl). But when I tried crack cocaine for the first time, it was a wrap! Nothing or no one else mattered. I acted as they did, but the crack was on the top of my list of priorities. I once heard someone say, *"When you're buying illegal or legal drugs on the streets, you're pseudo-suicidal because you're trusting the source selling it to you to be what he or she says it is.*" Any *"one"* of these drugs mentioned above could have been and probably should have led to my demise…BUT GOD! Although He had delivered me from drugs, I was still selling drugs. But I kept going to church. I felt guilty, but that didn't deter me from going to church. I knew God wasn't pleased with my continued behavior and activity of selling drugs, and God delivered me. I kept going to the altar. God wasn't finished with me just yet, because I was still drinking. Then, on Easter Sunday, April 20, 2003, I went down to the altar, and God delivered me from drinking too! What a mighty God we serve! I never imagined that God was preparing me to be a kidney donor to my brother in 2004. Amazingly, it would be exactly one year and four months later.

To God be the glory for all the things He's done in my life. In 2004, while attending a family meeting in Goldsboro, North Carolina, I asked my oldest brother a question. It had absolutely nothing to do with the gathering. *"Big Brother, how are you doing with your dialysis?"* He answered, *"I'm doing okay."* My brother, Pop, as we call him, speaks in a low, humble voice. It's a part of his demeanor. He also has a huge heart. He is a great brother to me and my siblings. He assumed the father-figure role at a young age because ours was absent.

I then asked, *"Do you need a kidney?"* Wow! I didn't know where that question came from! I wasn't planning to say that to him when I started the conversation. I now know that it was God speaking through me. *"Yes,"* he said, in his humble overtone. My next question and the response from me, I pray, will be pivotal for everyone reading this chapter. *"Why didn't you ask me!?"* I shall never forget the look in his eyes, as well as his reason for not asking me. *"I could never ask you for something like that."* At that moment, I thought to myself, *"How DO YOU ask someone to give you an organ out of their body!?"* The magnitude of asking such a question had never dawned on me. *How devastating would it be to hear someone say "no," especially from a family member or close friend!?* I'm sure both lives would be drastically impacted.

How many others, including myself, knew much about kidney dialysis? After being on the machine for a while, the kidney would function independently. To use a great quote, *"knowledge is power."* The love for my brother was apparent that day. My siblings and I agreed to get tested. We wanted to see if any of us were a match to become a donor. My Sister Sonia and I were compatible matches. She was deemed a better match. I asked her to allow me to donate my kidney to our brother. I felt this was part of God's plan for my life.

We had the transplant surgery on August 12, 2004. My brother's birthday is August 11, and what a celebration! He had just turned 55 years old the day before the surgery. I was 48 years old at the time. I included this to let someone know that it's never too late with God. In 2014, we celebrated his birthday and our 10th anniversary. We went to South Beach, Florida. On that day, I asked him, *"How have you been doing since the kidney transplant?"* Once again, I will never forget the look in his eyes or the response he gave me. *"I'm feeling good,"* he said, smiling. I asked him if he had any complications? He told me, "*No, none at all.*" He was still smiling. He asked me how I had been doing, and I told him that I was great! With a smile stretching from ear to ear, there was overwhelming joy and fulfillment at that moment. I then remembered the day of our surgery.

As I was coming from under the anesthesia, the doctor was standing over me. "*How are you feeling?*" he said. My response was, "*How is my brother doing?*" The doctor looked at me smiling and said, "*You both asked the same question when you came from under the anesthesia. He's doing fine.*" I smiled back. "*Did you write Redskins on the kidney, as I had requested*!?" (Yeah, my Big Brother likes that "*other*" team.) We both laughed. I could never explain or put into words how I felt that day. My brother and I had developed this bond and love for one another when we were kids. But what I can say is, PRAISE GOD! AND TO HIM I GIVE ALL THE GLORY! His timing is Awesome.

It was nothing but the blood of Jesus that saved and kept me! He was preparing me way before my brother needed a kidney. *How do I know this*? Because to be a kidney donor, you must go through extensive testing. They found no health issues in my body. This is why I was transparent and shared with you all the drugs I have put into my body! Even today, at 65 years old, I'm not diabetic, nor do I have high blood pressure. Even though these concerns run in my family, God is Awesome! He placed this vision in me to witness and encourage people—especially family members with loved ones on kidney dialysis.

I pray that the fear that may be stopping them from being tested will be removed in Jesus' Name. Amen. My big brother, Adrian "Pop" Powell, and I still like different teams. LOL And sometimes we go to games together. I love my brother and know he loves me. We tell each other all the time. I hope to become an advocate for kidney donors. I am providing education and first-hand information. By the way, testing and kidney surgery are free to the donor! *What if you needed a kidney? Wouldn't you want someone to help you by donating a kidney?*

One day while driving, God placed this quote in my thoughts, *"Don't let other people's opinions determine how you make decisions. The consequences you get are the results of the choices you make.* " This title, "God Gave Me Two Just In Case You Needed One," is something I wrote down years ago. Lord, please forgive me for all these years of procrastinating. And Lord, thank you for moving in Elder Nicole S. Mason and her husband, Mr. Sean Mason, to see something in me to invite me to share my story. Amen.

DEACON THOMAS G. WRIGHT

RAISED IN THE FIRE

There are times in life that come along to make you ponder your existence. The triumphs and successes coupled with the challenges and pitfalls can bring on deep introspection. *Why am I here? What is it all about? Will I accomplish the things assigned as my destiny?* You discover that the questions are not the problem. They often lead you to consider more issues to ponder that you didn't think of initially. It is the effort you put forth trying to unearth the answers that are really what can turn you upside down.

Approximately seventeen years ago, I was in with the doctor for my annual checkup and confided that for some reason, my heart was beating heavy at times. Those were the only words I had to explain this phenomenon. You see, I had reintroduced myself to the gym with one goal being to bench press 300 pounds, along with everything else I was doing. And this heavy heartbeat wasn't something that occurred all the time, but it also wasn't something that only happened in the gym. I was in my early thirties, but I was on a mission to get in *"shape,"* which means abs of steel and muscles bulging from under your clothes. The mission starts when men who have neglected their bodies pursue the Mr. Olympus goal upon viewing their unrecognizable image in every passing mirror.

I never got to that 300-pound weight - far from it, but I noticed that I'd be a little short of breath. My doctor listened to my chest and approved me to see a cardiologist to be on the safe side. That visit, unfortunately, was far from safe. This new doctor asked me a peculiar question. *"You ever had Rheumatic Fever?"* Of course, my simple reply was, *"I'm a Black male born and raised in*

D.C. - all we had were colds and the flu." No one in my family had been diagnosed with or met their demise because of their heart. I was the first one, though; that's not something to celebrate. He informed me I had Cardiac Myopathy, a Mitral Valve Prolapse, and a Dilated Aorta and that I should not be lifting anything above 25 pounds. *What??!!!* Recall when I stated that my heart was beating heavy? By now, you would've thought a Go-Go band was playing in my chest. Go-Go is a genre of music started in Washington, DC, that is heavy on the drums and percussion instruments.

The only question I had was, *"Am I dying?"* Fortunately, his response was a matter-of-fact no, but that I had to stop lifting weights and take medication for the rest of my days. It was that diagnosis, so I thought that gave me the answer to why I felt the way I did when I was in a heated situation. It was my heart acting up, not my feelings!! Again, so I thought.

I had another scare some years later when the doctor, examining me for ringing in my ear or Tinnitus and told me he saw a mass in my head. Here comes the Go-Go band again. I immediately thought of cancer, a condition that wreaks havoc. You see, cancer was a diagnosis that almost every person who had died in my family succumbed to. I naturally thought it was my turn. However, I did not accept the verdict my mind derived, but I was determined to believe God for the better! Some years had passed where I had accepted Christ as my Lord and Savior, and I was going to stand on God's Word come what may! I also had a praying wife, family, friends, Pastors, and church family. I wasn't supposed to be worried, but I could not seem to help it. The Go-Go band was in full swing. It was something that happened all day, every day, but it would come and go without reason. Yet, I recalled a prophet who had preached a revival at the church and called out my name. I wasn't there, but that did not stop him from prophesying that the enemy was trying to take me out with cancer but, the Lord said if my church family prayed, He'd spare my life. Well, I prayed, and so did my church family. And though I had major surgery to remove the mass from under my skull, it was not cancerous!

I gave you these episodes because they provide a glimpse of my reality. Yet, it may not be what you think. The medical events were undoubtedly some of the noted challenges and pitfalls of my life, but strangely, they were incidents that would lead me down a road toward triumphs and successes. (Stop scratching your head, and let me explain.) You see, I had a very dysfunctional childhood even though I didn't know it was that until I began to maturate towards manhood. My home life was filled with violence perpetrated by my father against my mother, sisters, and me. And my mother perpetrated her level of violence (they called it whippings) upon the children. We saw it as the daily occurrences of life in the hood, a hip word for the ghetto. I knew it was "*bad,*" if you will, but not different because most of the families I knew, including some of my extended family, were going through the same thing. It was a part of life, so I learned to live in and with it. What I didn't know at the time and what I began to understand is its far-reaching effects, both physical and mental.

While many homes were fatherless or places where the father visited infrequently, my house

159

was different. My father was present until I had just about reached my teen years. However, when you have the dysfunction regularly, the father figure's presence doesn't necessarily take away from it or fix it, but it can have the opposite effect of what one may think. My mother and father fought a lot. There was screaming, tussling, and blood!! Now, I'm not sure I was affected the most because I was the youngest of four in the house. I only know how it made me feel. Besides me and the sister closest to me comparing whelps from the occasional extension cord beating we had just received, we never discussed it. That is one of the core principles of dysfunction. You don't discuss it. Another critical principle of dysfunction was the notion of, "W*hat happens in this house stays in the house!*" The problem with these principles is that you often don't learn the detrimental effects they have on you until later in life.

Due to the dysfunction, there were drugs in my life, and only by the grace of God am I here! The one thing I can say is that self-medication never works in the grand scheme of things; at least, I've never seen it work. You can never bury it

160

deep enough without "*it*" (whatever your it is), having a devastating effect on you whether you know it or admit it. Growing up in a violent household can cause you to accept violence from others in your relationships or divvy it out. Unless you deal with it, it will rear its ugly head in ways you dare not imagine. I learned that mine was panic attacks. I'll tell you about that later.

The dysfunction came to a head when my father shot at my mother in the presence of my cousin. And, although I wasn't there when it happened, it felt like I was there, hearing the loud "BANG!!" and I was frozen!!! I had this feeling aching feeling listening to my cousin recount the story. Wait!! "*Is that the Go-Go sound I'm hearing, feeling in my chest?*" Yes, there came a time when I recall hearing, feeling my heart beating that heavy beat! Thank God my father missed my mother and my cousin. Unfortunately, that wasn't the end of the ordeal. When the bullets didn't hit my mother, and the gun jammed, my father then beat my mother with the gun. And he beat her badly. Keeping all of this information "*in the* house" had a very warped sense of direction. What I do know and now understand is how it affected me.

I pontificated (love that word) about two of the medical dramas that I endured, but there were others. Sometimes I wonder how so many different issues can affect one person. I've asked the Lord that very same question numerous times, yet His response became a settling 2 Corinthians 12:9. *"My grace is sufficient for thee: for my strength is made perfect in weakness."* (KJV) Yes, His grace is sufficient, but to me, that means, He has given me the strength to face adversity and deal with issues that make life worth living. I had to come to grips and deal with issues from my past about my family and my father. I prayed, cried, shouted, and danced over the problems, only for them to be right there when I finished. I wanted to help others and not be bothered to help myself. The Lord knew what I needed, and He caused it to be in my life in the strangest of ways.

My health insurance has a program that seeks patients who can use coaching, counseling, or therapy to help cope with long-standing medical issues. When they initially contacted me, I rejected them. *"I don't need no mental help!!"* yet all along, I knew I did. Fortunately, they were persistent, and I soon relented with the thought of, *"What can it hurt?"* I faked myself out with the notion that I was okay because I had Christ in my life, and He was all I needed. Sadly, many Born Again believers think the same way, and what I've discovered is that a large number of them are men. Women seem to have a way of releasing and trusting in specific processes whereby men believe it is an insult to their manhood. We were told to shake it off and tough it out, and the most common, *"MEN DON'T CRY!"* So, we walk around with this ball of knots and pain and despair, and sometimes when it is released, we wind up on the wrong side of the law or the wrong side of drug addiction or relationship or many other things that I'm sure you don't need me to name. **Brothers, we must get free**!! *How can the Lord honestly use us for ministry or simply enjoy life when we are afraid for the Holy Spirit, whether directly or indirectly, to minister to us?* The same effort I put into being free, truly free with my wife and

163

kids, is the same effort I had to put into being free with myself.

I gave it a chance because I thought it was all about my physical health, yet I started the sessions with little expectation. It was hard to release even with the words at the tip of my tongue. I had to learn to trust, and that was hard! Over the years, I learned to trust men close to me. It was hard because I believe my early life with my father played a significant factor. As much as I wanted, I only recall having a strained relationship with him from my youth. I had friends that were/are close, but they are longstanding relationships. One best friend I've known since we were babies because our mothers were like sisters. I have another I've known since kindergarten, which is excellent considering he recalls things about me in elementary school that I've forgotten. Unfortunately, I don't remember a great deal of my childhood which can be pretty disheartening. I had no issue trusting women. I had no problem relating to women, but maybe that's because they had what I wanted, and I was pretty good at getting it.

Anyway, I learned to trust brothers as I grew into manhood, but not many. Strangely, when I gave my life to Christ in my late twenties, I lost most of my male friends. Not my two brothers from childhood, but the rest fell away. It was hard to have relationships when I was going one way, and they were going in another direction. Fortunately, the Lord provided me with friends, brothers in my church fellowship. I learned to trust brothers and gained lifelong friendships. There is a Scripture that comes to mind which states, *"A man that hath friends must shew himself friendly: and there is a friend that sticketh closer than a brother."* Proverbs 18:24 (KJV)

After I joined the church, I attended and soon conducted men's rap sessions with Christian brothers who needed other men to share and care; not give the cookie-cutter answers to the many issues that concern us. Trust comes in many different forms, and it is a hard thing to give, but you must trust to be free. You must trust the Lord with all your heart, soul, and mind to see yourself as He sees you. My physical ailments brought me to counseling, but my mental health kept me coming back. I had a coach who taught me breathing lessons that help with anxiety or panic attacks. My counseling sessions helped clear away just enough hurdles and blockages to hear and receive the information being offered. I suspected having anxiety but could never articulate it. It was fear though fear could be a trigger, not the result. The sessions with the counselor and the life coach confirmed what I probably knew all along but would never admit.

I have anxiety, but I believed it was essential to probe why I have this condition. I surmise that it's like going to a doctor, and he only treats the symptoms, so he gives you a prescription. Yeah, the pills help, but they don't cure. I wanted to get to the why and, perhaps, deal with it to no longer require treatment for the symptom because the problem is healed. I believed it was worth a try.

Moreover, I came to myself realizing that I could not church it away. If that were the case, I would've stopped having the episodes a long time ago. Being in fellowship with others is good, and having quality relationships with men I trust and trust me has also been good. But I

166

knew that sometimes a professional is needed for treatment. Yes, my relationship with the Lord plays a significant factor in my mental well-being. Salvation or my walk with the Lord opened me to who I am and who I use to be. He deals with the things, the improper pieces of one's life, and provides the opportunity to deal with them. He takes the things you least expect or stuff you did not know was buried and uses them to heal you as you heal others. *"And they overcame him by the blood of the Lamb, and by the word of their testimony; and they loved not their lives unto the death."* Revelation 12:11 (KJV)

I'm sure you know incidents from your childhood can have a resounding effect on the adult you become. Perhaps, you were more competent and more in tune than I but, I learned (and am still learning) or at least now understand the effect violence had on me. It is called Childhood Trauma, and many suffer from it. I believe it is analogous to Post Traumatic Stress Disorder or PTSD. It can take on many forms and exhibit various mannerisms, behaviors, and thoughts. While it can manifest as something mild or severe, treatment is available for one's betterment. So many things I did were probably symptoms of the trauma. I did many foolish things that could've landed me in prison or a morgue, but I believe the Lord covered me for some reason. Of course, He knew what I was doing and why I was doing it because He is omniscient or knows everything. I certainly don't hold myself up as better than anyone who was punished for their deeds, but I am thankful that He spared me! Perhaps, He intended to use my story, my life, to help another brother or sister who went through or is going through a similar existence. If that be the case, I accept the task.

My father and I now have a great relationship. My first and only trip with him was to a Manpower Conference with Bishop T.D. Jakes in Atlanta, Georgia. To help my wife and me, my father would pick up my two younger sons from elementary school and take them home because of our work schedule. He and my mother were able to be in the same room again. They were cordial to one another, AND she let him in her home and fed him if food were being served. Oh, let me just tell you that my mother, sister, cousin, niece, and nephew followed suit after I got saved. My sons grew up in a home different than my childhood home. I saw the miracles my God could do with my own eyes, and I'm still amazed. However, although the trauma is long past, I still had to contend with the attacks. Only now can I put a rationale to it. I continue in my treatment in hopes of beating it. It will take perseverance, effort, and a will to get to the finish line. I am up for the challenge.

I tell you my story not to garner any semblance of sympathy or to draw the proverbial "*pat on the back*" because I made it through the madness. I tell you this as a testimony of the greatness of the God that I serve and the revelation that if I made it, so can you. I'm nothing special. I made many choices, and a great deal of them were not good. I STILL wonder to this day, "*Why me?*" "*Why did I end up at my church or link up with people I found to be just like me, sinners saved by grace?*" "*Why did the Lord pluck me up and shield me from death or destruction while others I knew perished?*" The only answer I have and that makes any sense to me is Jesus.

My children are loved. The love that my wife and I share is the complete opposite of what I witnessed as a child. I've been employed by the Federal Government going on 40 years. I started at the bottom, even with a bachelor's degree, to get my foot in the door. I worked my way up to a position for which I was never trained and began making an income sufficient to sustain my family and me. I joined a congregation of believers and left behind the life of pure evil when I accepted Jesus Christ as my Lord and Savior and chose to sit under the tutelage of my current Pastors, Archbishop Alfred A. Owens, Jr., and Dr. Susie C. Owens.

I often wonder, did I really choose or did I ever have a choice. The Scripture reads, *"choose ye this day who you will serve,"* but were the things I saw and heard and lived make that move more of destiny to get to this place so I can tell someone that, you too, can make it!? *How does this end?* I may never be able to wear the half shirt to show my non-existent rock-hard abs, nor will the shirt be too tight to highlight my bulging muscles, but I'm on my way to a healthy mind, if not a completely healthy body.

The Fire (dysfunction) in which one is Raised does not have to kill, maim, or cripple you, but for that to happen, you have to face some truths that must be revealed, and maybe even a counselor to guide you through the process. I can relay to you that it is very accurate that your chances of success will exponentially increase when you allow the Lord in it. He will see you through it!

MEET THE CO-AUTHORS

Steve Alsbrooks

S. Vernon Alsbrooks is a native of Columbus, Ohio. He attended Marion-Franklin High School and matriculated to Washington, DC, to attend Howard University on a football scholarship. While at Howard, Steve pledged and became a member of the distinguished men of Kappa Alpha Psi Fraternity Incorporated. After college, Steve gave his life to Jesus the Christ.

In 1986, Steve joined the DC Metropolitan Police Department. During his tenure, Steve rose to the rank of Master Patrol Officer. He served as Chief Shop Steward for the Second Police District. He retired in 2011. After retirement, he went back to law enforcement from 2013 until the present. He is a Greater Mount Calvary Holy Church member under the leadership of Bishop Alfred and Co-Pastor Susie Owens. He has served on multiple ministries, the Security

Ministry and Men's Prayer Group Ministry that he started.

In 2013, Steve created a community program entitled *"Survival Skills When Stopped by the Police."* Steve is married to the love of his life, Evangelist Carol Alsbrooks. They have been married for 30 years. They are the proud parents of two sons, Aaron and Andrew.

Deacon Edward "Leon" Best

Deacon Leon is a native Washingtonian and was educated in the DC Public Schools. Like so many young men, his academic career started so strong that it garnered him a full scholarship to a College Preparatory High School in Amenia, New York. He then began his college studies at Saint Augustine's College in Raleigh, North Carolina.

He is a public servant, working as a shining light as a bus operator for Metro. He serves as a proud member of the Deacon Board at the Greater Mount Calvary Holy Church. He credits God for directing him to his church and, more specifically, into a relationship with his Pastor, Archbishop Alfred Owens, Jr.

Deacon Leon is married to the love of his life, Angie, and they are the proud parents of a huge family. He chooses not to use the term "half-brothers, sisters or blended families." Instead, he chooses to focus on showing and expressing unconditional, compassionate, and understanding love to his family and expects the same from all of their children and grandchildren.

Elder Tony Keith, Sr.

Tony Keith is an ordained Elder at Greater Mt. Calvary Holy Church, Washington, DC, under Archbishop Alfred A. Owens, Jr., and Dr. Susie C. Owens. He faithfully serves on the Ministerial Alliance, the Divorce Care Ministry, the Marriage Enrichment Ministry, and the National Adjutancy Academy.

Elder Tony is an Intern Marriage & Family Therapist with Sonja Williams & Associates, LLC serving Prince Georges and Montgomery County, MD. As a therapist, he gravitates towards using solution-focused therapy, narrative therapy, and structural family therapy incorporating cultural/environmental influences. Some areas of interest include working with blended families, communication in the relationship, issues associated with infidelity in the marriage, and issues related to substance abuse.

This retired U.S. Air Force veteran has endured many battle wounds, yet he has emerged as a clear victor! Now, he carries his scars as badges of honor. He helps married couples to change their "stuck story" and take charge of their lives and their marriage with clarity and confidence.

As CEO and Founder of Tony Keith Ministries, Elder Tony uses his failures and his 20+ years of marriage to help engaged and married couples live out their purpose, leverage their experiences, and maximize their potential in their relationships. Through his coaching, mentoring, and live speaking events, he teaches biblical principles that will inspire you to shift into high gear; help you get rid of what's standing in your way; and empower you to maintain your momentum! As clients rediscover their identity and embrace their authenticity, they are transformed from sitting to soaring in their marriages and personal lives!

He has been a speaker in both church and secular platforms transforming lives through self-discovery and change. In his quest to become a Licensed Clinical Marriage & Family Therapist (LCMFT), Elder Tony is presently pursuing his master's degree in Marriage & Family Therapy from Capella University, Minneapolis, MN. He has an undergraduate degree in Christian Counseling from National Bible College & Seminary, Ft. Washington, MD, and studied Pastoral Care and Counseling extensively at Wesley Theological Seminary, Washington, DC.

Elder Tony formerly served as the Program Coordinator of the Greater Mt. Calvary Holy Church, Prison Ministry, Reintegration Support Group Initiative for returning offenders. He also served the DC General Health Campus, Detoxification Center, Washington, DC, where he provided coaching and inspirational support to those participating in the Substance Abuse Treatment Program. Elder Tony is a Student Member of the American Association of Marriage and Family Therapy (AAMFT), and a

Presidential Member of the American Association of Christian Counselors (AACC).

Elder Tony is married to Lady Starlean (Lyons) Keith, and together they host some of the most power-fun-conversational events on relationship building. They are a blended family and proud parents of four adult children and six grandchildren. His grandchildren add life to his years and years to his life.

Sean P. Mason

Sean P. Mason is the Founder and CEO of Capital Gaming Studios, LLC., founded in 2018. He has ten years of gaming and event experience. As a District of Columbia Lottery Board manager, his sales team was responsible for $50 million of annual lottery sales. He also coordinated over 100 local events a year through partnerships, including The National Auto Show, The National Bar b Que Battle, Washington Wizards, and the Washington Nationals sporting events, to name a few.

Sean has been a top sales producer in Finance, Real Estate, and Government Sales. Sensing a need to close the digital divide between the majority and underrepresented communities, Sean founded Capital Gaming Studios, LLC; a Tech Company focused on Esports: gaming, game and video development, coding, and entrepreneurship. His company explicitly targets inner-city youth with league-type style and tournament play. He has begun to develop gaming laboratories in elementary and middle schools where students are taught and encouraged to embrace and exercise their creative genius freely.

Capital Gaming Studios LLC was awarded the contract to operate and develop the Winter Esports League for KIPP DC Charter Schools (Benning Heights Campus). Capital Gaming Studios LLC., was the lead consultant on a STEM Grant for KIPP DC and was awarded $25,000 to obtain gaming computers. Capital Gaming Studios, LLC opened the very first Gaming Laboratory in Washington, DC, in 2019.

He holds a Bachelor of Science from Howard University. Sean was awarded a full athletic scholarship, serving as one of the noted team leaders of the varsity basketball team during his tenure. For his accomplishments, Sean was inducted into the Howard University Sports Hall of Fame in 2016.

He is married to Dr. Nicole S. Mason. They are the proud parents of three sons and two daughters. Their family recently expanded with two grandchildren.

Alvin Owens

A native Washingtonian, Alvin was born and raised in the District of Columbia. He serves as Chairman of the Trustee Board at Greater Mt. Calvary Holy Church and has an "undercover" Nursing Home Ministry. Alvin began his career as a Sky Marshall for the Federal Aviation Administration at Washington National Airport, receiving his training at the FBI Academy in Glenco, GA. Taking advantage of the educational opportunities, he served five years as a Law Enforcement Officer at the airport and took training to become a Heavy Diesel Engine Repair Mechanic. He served in that position for seven years. Taking further advantage of educational opportunities, Alvin became a Locksmith, eventually becoming the Lead

Locksmith at the airport, and still holds that position.

Alvin has worked at Ronald Reagan Washington National Airport for over forty years. In addition, Alvin is also a licensed Real Estate Agent and was a member of the first graduating class of Calvary Bible Institute, earning a Certificate in Biblical Studies. Alvin has a unique ability to bring joy to everyone he comes in contact with and make people laugh. He loves listening and singing to music and enjoys spending time with family. Alvin has been married to his wife, Barbara, for 29 years and has a Daughter, Tykia, a Son, Michael, and two Grandchildren, Kynley and Brion.

Elder Anthony Pender

Anthony L. Pender is a native Washingtonian and a product of D.C. Public Schools. After graduation, he entered the field of Healthcare Administration. He is a 30-year Health Care professional currently serving as Dues Billing Manager. In 1997 he joined the Greater Mt Calvary Holy Church of Washington, DC. He serves in the capacity of an Elder. He and his wife, Helen, are currently serving as leaders of the Family Ministry. He also serves as an instructor for the church's Discipleship Class and one of the instructors for the Marriage Enrichment Ministry. Anthony is a big believer in healthy families and marriages.

Anthony also earned an Executive Certificate in Leadership and Management from Notre Dame in 1996. In September 2017, Anthony answered the call from God to go back to school to complete his education. He graduated in May 2021 with his Bachelor of Business Administration from Lancaster Bible College. He is also a graduate of Calvary Bible Institute.

Anthony shares life and ministry with his wife, Helen Pender, to whom he has been married since 1994. Together they have two beautiful daughters Bria and Brittany. One of his favorite scriptures can be found in Psalms 34:1, "*I will bless the Lord at all times, his praise shall continually be in my mouth.*"

Minister Bernard Perry

Minister Bernard Perry hails from Smyrna, Georgia. He is the 7th of eight children born to the late Sergeant John T. and Earlene Ross Perry. Minister Perry holds a Bachelor of Science Degree from Howard University and a Master of Arts Degree from Trinity University.

While attending Howard, he was a four-year starter on the Men's Basketball team from 1979-1983. Drafted by the Washington Bullets in 1983, his professional career was shortened by an injury. In 2003, Howard University acknowledged his contributions to the basketball program by inducting him into the Howard University Hall of Fame. Minister Perry is a proud member of Phi Beta Sigma Fraternity, Inc. He has been a member for over 30 years.

He is currently employed by the Prince George's County Public School System. He has been married to his college sweetheart, Mrs. Edana Johnson Perry, for 35 years. They are the proud parents of three children Taelor, Christian, Kayla, and the proud grandparents to Ariyah and Amahri.

Minister Perry and his wife serve as members of the Family Ministry at Greater Mt. Calvary Holy Church (GMCHC). He also serves as Vice President of the Men's Ministry. For over eight years, he and his wife also served as parent facilitators for the clients of the Family Reunification Program (co-sponsored by the D.C.-based Court Service Offender Supervision Agency (CSOSA) and GMCHC. As a mentor to hundreds of young people, Minister Perry credits God, his family, his Pastors, Bishop Alfred Owens, and Co-Pastor Susie Owens, as well as Phi Beta Sigma Fraternity, Inc. with influencing him to become the man he is today.

Russell Roy

Russell Roy, Jr was born May 3, 1967, in Washington, DC; to the incredible parents Russell and Cordelia Roy; raised in Capital Heights, MD.; attended public schools in both the District of Columbia and Prince George's County, Maryland.

He has been married to his queen Kimberly Roy for 30 years, and they have two beautiful daughters: Shadae (23) and Janae (20).

184

In 1989, Russell enlisted in the United States Army and served as a Military Police, traveling to many countries to support military training and combat. He is a veteran of the Persian Gulf War - Desert Storm. He fulfilled his military obligation at the rank of Staff Sergeant.

In 1989, he became a Greater Mt. Calvary Holy Church member. In 1990, just before being deployed to fight in the Gulf War, he accepted Jesus Christ as his Lord and Savior.

Upon returning home, he enrolled in barbering school and earned his District of Columbia Barber's License. Two years later, he successfully passed the master's barber examination. He also joined Calvary's Male Chorus, and months later, his Pastor, Bishop Owens, appointed him to serve on the Trustee Board. Russell and Bishop developed a close relationship in this role. Russell soon became his Bishop's personal barber and continues to do so today.

Russell's love for cutting hair led him to tap into his entrepreneurial interest, and in 2000 Cross Cuts Barbershop was born. Russell now has over

20 years of barbershop ownership and management experience. Although his pastor told Russell that he had a calling on his life to preach, Russell chose to make his barber chair his pulpit. Here, he listens and attempts to show compassion and offer Godly sound advice to those who have an open heart to receive it.

Over the past ten years, Russell has had the honor and privilege of serving as an active participant, contributor, and educator for the Greater Mt. Calvary Holy Church Son's ministry, a ministry for young men from single parent households.

Russell started his government career as a Clerk-Typist, refusing to settle for an entry-level position. Russell worked very hard to achieve the requirements for the next level, and for the next 13 years, Russell would be promoted to various positions. And in 1997, Russell became the National Park Service's first African American Special Agent and retired after 35 years in 2019 as the first African American Chief of the Investigative Services Branch.

Throughout his career, Russell was promoted based on his skills, attitude, and ability to work well with others; not having a college degree quickly challenged his credentials among his peers. In 2001, Russell went on to earn several degrees to strengthen his professional credentials. In 2001, he completed his Associate Degree in Business Management from Prince George's Community College. In 2011, he earned his bachelor's degree in Management and Leadership from Johns Hopkins University. In 2012, he earned his master's degree in Management and Leadership from Johns Hopkins University.

To further expand his entrepreneurial interest, he and his wife created a real estate investment business. They purchase distressed homes, renovating and transforming the property into someone's dream home and/or rental homes across multiple states.

Russell's most important job is being a father to his daughters and a King to his Queen, but without Christ, his bio would simply be a blank piece of paper at the center of his life.

Deacon Daryl Shambourger

Born in the City of Brotherly Love, Philadelphia, PA, Deacon Daryl Shambourger made his way to Washington, DC, to attend Howard University. Shortly after that, he found employment with Georgetown University's Athletic Department - Finance Office. He was later transferred to the Men's Basketball Office under the late Coach, John Thompson, Jr.

He credits his loving parents for their guidance which helped him to become the man he is today. Daryl was greatly impacted by the intervention sessions in the kitchen of Mother Charlotte McCoy.

Daryl later settled into a career in Security. While working as a security officer, he obtained a certification as an Emergency Medical Technician. Daryl has a servant's heart, always looking to render services to others. He has been a member of Greater Mount Calvary Holy Church since 2003 under the leadership of Archbishop Alfred Owens and Co-Pastor Susie Owens. He has served with numerous ministries and is presently a facilitator with the Discipleship Ministry.

Daryl is married to Nicole Shamburger, his queen, a wonderfully supportive wife, and friend. He is also the proud father to his daughter Nia Shambourger.

Deacon Thomas G. Wright

Deacon Thomas G. Wright is a proud native son of Washington, DC. He attended DC public schools and completed his primary education at Gonzaga College High School. He attended the University of Maryland, College Park, and graduated in 1981. Thomas has a Bachelor of Arts degree in Criminology.

Employed with the U.S. Department of Justice since 1982, he is currently an Information Technology Manager for the Solicitor General and Office of Legal Counsel. He has been a member of Greater Mt. Calvary Holy Church since 1987. Shortly after joining the church, he accepted Jesus Christ as his Lord and Savior.

Deacon Wright and his wife Paula have been married since 1990. They are blessed with two sons, Thomas Alexander, and Christian Charles, 28 and 25 years old, respectively. Deacon Wright is also the father of 31-year-old Evan James. Saved, sanctified, and Holy Ghost filled, he is dedicated to the will of the Lord, the ways of his family, and the work of the ministry.

Deacon Thomas is an active member of Greater Mt. Calvary Holy Church, not just in word but also in deed. An ordained Deacon since 1989, he currently serves as Chairman of the Deacon Board, leading over 50 men. He also serves on the Men of Valor Executive Board, his church's Men's Ministry. For several years, Deacon Thomas was a member of *"Set the Captives Free"* Prison Ministry and once served as Assistant Coordinator. He taught his first class in the accredited Calvary Bible Institute in 1996 and soon became a fixture of its faculty. He currently authors or selects other men to write the Men's Column for the *The Greater – The Magnificent View Magazine*, the online magazine of Greater Mount Calvary Holy Church. His major task in life is to be the best husband, father, man, and servant the Lord has called him to be.

The Scripture he lives by is Matthew 6:33, *"But seek ye first the kingdom of God, and His righteousness; and all these things shall be added unto you."*

ABOUT THE VISIONARY
DR. NICOLE S. MASON, ESQUIRE

Born with a spirit of advocacy, Nicole knew at the age of 9 that she wanted to be a lawyer. Having what she felt was the "gift of gab," Nicole would speak up for those that either wouldn't or couldn't speak up for themselves. She has carried this same energy into her adult life. In addition to her advocacy, Nicole is a bold, courageous, and confident woman on a mission to help other women to live life and achieve success on their own terms.

As an only child and working in her grandmother's dry cleaners, Nicole is an astute businesswoman. Her grandmother pushed her to go after her dream of becoming a lawyer, but when it came time for her to apply to law school, she applied nine times and was rejected nine times. Yes, you read that correctly. She was rejected nine times. She would not take no for an answer. She applied for the 10th time and was accepted. Upon entering the orientation, some of Nicole's classmates gasped for air. They were shocked and surprised to see Nicole big, round, and pregnant and starting law school! She graduated on time with her class and passed the bar exam.

Nicole is the owner of a boutique law firm specializing in Estate Planning. She also operates a coaching and speaking business. She intentionally uses her skills, talents, and skills in the earth and being a blessing to others.

Sensing the call on her life to preach the Gospel of Jesus Christ, Nicole quit her job and immersed herself in her studies at Howard University School of Divinity. During her tenure, she was selected to serve as the Faculty Research Scholar for the esteemed Old Testament Professor, Dr. Gene Rice. Nicole was also the recipient of more than $20,000 in scholarships while matriculating at the Divinity School.

Nicole has always spoken her truth and has been a trailblazer in her career. She has served as the first and only African American to serve in her position of an Equal Employment Opportunity/Diversity and Inclusion professional for her organization. She has been the recipient of many awards in this capacity and continues to blaze trails in her industry. She has worked in this area for more than 30 years.

Nicole started her ministry, SISTERGRAM Ministries, in 1998 with a newsletter and a circulation of approximately 125 women in her then local church. In less than two years, the newsletter circulation had grown to more than 2,000 women across the country and in various prisons. Nicole has used her gift of writing to encourage women over the past 20 years. She was honored in October 2018 by the Governor of Maryland for her work with women over the years.

In addition to her writing gift, Nicole held a monthly fellowship for women for 12 years, ministering to more than 1,000 women over that time. She has also hosted a weekly prayer call for the past 15 years and continues to do so today.

Nicole has hosted her own international online show reaching viewers around the world. She also hosted her own radio show on Urban One, formerly Radio One.

She is an international best-selling author who wrote four books of her own and served as a contributing writer in more than 30 book projects. She is the recipient of the prestigious 2018 50 Great Writers You Should Be Reading Contest. Her very first anthology, *Faith For Fiery Trials: Testimonies That Will Ignite The Fire In Your Soul And Increase Your Faith In God*, was the 2019 Anthology of the Year presented by the Indie Author Legacy Awards in partnership with Black Enterprise. Nicole was also a finalist for Female Author of the Year and a finalist for the Reader's Choice Award. Her books have been highlighted in several countries: South Africa, South American, Australia, Netherlands, to name a few. She is also a monthly contributing writer several magazines. Nicole was also selected as the 2019 ACHI Woman of the Year. She was also selected as the #SpeakerCon Faith Based Speaker of the Year for 2019.

Nicole is a mentor and a leader's leader, serving as coach and confidante to many high-achieving women in ministry and the marketplace. Women look to her for spiritual guidance and Godly wisdom for everyday living. She is an Executive Leadership Coach serving women leaders in the marketplace. She holds a Bachelor of Arts in Sociology from Howard University, a Juris Doctor from the University of the District of Columbia David A. Clarke School of Law, a Master of Law Degree in Litigation and Dispute Resolution from the George Washington University School of Law, and a Master of Divinity from Howard University School of Divinity. She also has a Certificate in Leadership Coaching from Georgetown University and is a Certified Speaker, Trainer, and Coach with the John Maxwell Team.

She is an Ambassador for the American Heart Association, turning her pain into purpose. Having lost her Mom to heart disease and being diagnosed shortly after her mother passed away, Nicole has been intentional about spreading the message to other African American women about heart health awareness. Nicole was featured in a commercial sharing her Mom's story and her story on more than 12 media outlets in various magazines, newsletters, and jumbotrons at multiple airports.

Nicole completed the Women in Leadership Program at the prestigious Brookings Institute. She also completed the first Women's Leadership Program at her alma mater, George Washington University. Nicole is a professional speaker certified by the National Speakers Association. She is a member of the International Coach Federation, Maryland Bar Association, National Association of Professional Women, and Federally Employed Women (FEW).

She currently serves as an Equal Employment Opportunity/Diversity Program Manager at the US Department of Commerce/NOAA Research. She is the recipient of NOAA's highest award for the first Diversity Summit in the Agency's history. She served as a Chapter President and the National Vice President for Compliance for FEW. During her Presidency, the Chapter was recognized for increasing membership and Community Outreach Projects offering "Comfy Chemo Bags" to women undergoing chemotherapy and "Dress For Success," offering business attire to underprivileged individuals returning to the workforce.

Nicole has spoken at numerous conferences, both sacred and secular, including the Success Women's Conference held in Biloxi, MS, alongside Lisa Nichols and other notable speakers and influencers, Washington Suburban Sanitary Commission (WSSC) Women In Business Conference, American Mothers National Conference, Federally Employed Women's National Training Program, to name a few, making impact on every platform. She is a world changer destined to help women Show Up Great, Speak Up With Confidence and Stand Out Courageously!

OTHER BOOKS AND PROJECTS BY NICOLE S. MASON

Faith For Fiery Trials: Testimonies That Will Ignite The Fire In Your Soul And Increase Your Faith In God

Maintain Your Momentum: Success Quotes for High Achieving Women

Monday Morning Motivations: Encouraging Words to Start Your Week

Morning Meditations: Starting Your Day with Passion, Purpose, and Power

Meditaciones Matinales: Comenzando Tu Dia Con Proposito Pasión Y Poder

CONTRIBUTING AUTHOR IN
THE FOLLOWING BOOKS

Chicken Soup for the Soul®: Miracles & Divine
Intervention – 101 Stories of Faith and Hope
Presented By Amy Newmark

You Are Enough! Messages of Inspiration &
Empowerment To Live Your Best Life
Presented By Les Brown And Dr. Cheryl Wood

Live Your Faith Out Loud: Real-life Stories
Compelling You to do More!
Presented By Dorothy Patrick Wilson

I Am A Victor!: Stories of individuals who
victoriously turned their pain into purpose
Presented By Dr. Cheryl Wood

The Unstoppable Warrior Woman: Inspirational Stories of Women Who Overcame the Odds and Chose to Thrive
Presented By Bershan Shaw

Glambitious Guide To Win in 2021
An Ebook Presented By Glam Boss Organization

Speaking My Truth: 50 Real Life Stories That Inspire, Empower, Heal and Transform
Presented By Cheryl Wood

Beyond Inspiration: 14 Transformational Prayers To Increase Your Impact and Influence
Presented By Melissa J. Nixon

Daily Dose of Declarations: A 365 Day Journey To Help You Declare Positive Affirmations Over Your Life
Presented By Melanie Bonita

The Breaking To Brilliance: 15 Powerful Stories Of Triumph and Healing
Presented By Dr. Valeka Moore

No More Chains – It's Time For Change: 11 Real Life Transformations Empowering You To

Release Mental, Emotional, and Generational
Chains
Presented By Ari Squires

Voices of the 21st Century: Women Who
Influence, Inspire and Make a Difference
Presented by Nicole S. Mason and Nicole S.
Mason

Glambitious Guide To Win in 2019
An Ebook Presented By Glam Boss Organization

Push Through: How The Process Leads To The
Promise
An Ebook Presented By Glam Boss Organization

What Is A Courageous Woman: A Collaborative
Book Featuring 78 Co-Authors Celebrating
Courageous Women
Presented By Telishia Berry

Glambitious Guide To Greatness: How To Go
From Doubt To Destiny & From Surviving To
Thriving
An E-book Presented By Glam Boss
Organization

Behind The Scenes of a Phenomenal Woman:
Featuring Stories of 24 Phenomenal Women
Presented By Dr. Chantelle Teasdell

Women Inspiring Nations: 25 Women Sharing
Their Stories and Gifts to Inspire and Transform
Lives Across Nations
Presented By Cheryl Wood

Igniting the Fire: A Woman's Guide to Setting a
Blaze in Ministry, Business, and Life
Presented By LaTracey Copeland Hughes

The Fearless Living Experience: Bold and
Empowered Women Share Their Triumph Over
Life's Curveballs
Presented By Cheryl Wood

Made in the USA
Middletown, DE
16 June 2021